THE ART OF WAR

G

THE
ART OF WAR
FOR
DATING

MASTER SUN TZU'S TACTICS
TO WIN OVER WOMEN

ERIC ROGELL, the guy behind TheBachelorGuy.com

Avon, Massachusetts

Published by
Adams Media, a division of F+W Media, Inc.
57 Littlefield Street, Avon, MA 02322. U.S.A.
www.adamsmedia.com

ISBN 10: 1-4405-0668-X
ISBN 13: 978-1-4405-0668-0
eISBN 10: 1-4405-1174-8
eISBN 13: 978-1-4405-1174-5

Printed in the United States of America.

10   9   8   7   6   5   4   3   2

Library of Congress Cataloging-in-Publication Data
Rogell, Eric.
The art of war for dating / Eric Rogell.
p. cm.
Includes index.
ISBN-13: 978-1-4405-0668-0
ISBN-10: 1-4405-0668-X
ISBN-13: 978-1-4405-1174-5 (ebk)
ISBN-10: 1-4405-1174-8 (ebk)
1. Dating (Social customs) 2. Interpersonal relations. 3. Strategic planning.
4. Sunzi, 6th cent. B.C. I. Title.
HQ801.R625 2011
646.7'7081—dc22
2010039868

This book is available at quantity discounts for bulk purchases.
For information, please call 1-800-289-0963.

DEDICATION

For every guy who ever thought he wasn't good looking enough, smart enough, rich enough, or anything else enough to date incredible women. The truth is they're waiting for you. Stop sitting around and get out there.

ACKNOWLEDGMENTS

As much as I'd love to take credit for everything, a work of brilliance with this kind of staggering insight and information doesn't happen without the help of a lot of other people. Like Brendan O'Neill, my editor, who not only conceived this book, but championed me as its author, provided a much-needed sounding board to bounce my (sometimes outrageous) ideas off of, and expertly guided me through a much more complex process than I could ever have imagined. Chris Illuminati of TheNoobDad.com, who had the foresight to introduce Brendan to my work. Katie Corcoran Lytle, whose keen editing eye and ingenious suggestions kept me on track and lead to a book that makes me look far more intelligent than I should. Cheryl Charming and Dr. Stephanie Sarkis, veterans of too many books to count, for giving me an author's view of what to expect, and encouraging me along the way. My agent June Clark, who dealt with the details and always had my back so I could focus on my keyboard. And Bobby Rio, who provided an invaluable amount of research and resources.

And thanks to my mother, Joan, the strongest and most caring woman in the world, for teaching me that women are always to be respected, and my father, Les, for showing me that doesn't mean you can't have fun with them. Erin Nicole, my little girl who even to this day has stolen my heart like no other woman could ever hope to. To close friends like Andy Moes, John and Josh Nye, Clark Trainor, Adam Eckstein, and many others, whose endless questions and genuine desire to be better men lead to the creation of The Bachelor Guy, and ultimately this book. And a special thank you to: Lynn, because you never forget your first; Gaye who showed me feisty can be just as sexy as sweet can be; Barbara who taught me more about love and life than any woman before or since; Donna Lee who demonstrated that even drunken Spring Break hook-ups can turn into life-long friendships; and Christine who proved that great friends can indeed become great lovers. You all have a special place in my heart; along with every other woman I ever dated, you've made me a better man.

CONTENTS

INTRODUCTION

"Most of us are pawns in a game of love we don't understand."

—Leo F. Buscalia

"You have to learn the rules of the game. And then you have to play better than anyone else."

—Albert Einstein

Have you ever had an epiphany? You know, one of those "ah-ha" moments when a light bulb suddenly snaps on in your brain, and your eyes open to a realization that sticks with you for the rest of your life?

Yeah, me too.

And it happened the first time I tried to reach second base.

No, not *that* second base. (Although there were many epiphanies that happened there too.) I'm talking about *the* second base; the square, white bag, between first base and third base. I was in first grade, and we were playing kickball during one of our first gym classes.

At that time, the sum total of my knowledge of kickball was as follows: You stand at home plate and the gym teacher slowly rolls a big red ball to you. You kick that thing as hard as you can and run to first base before the ball gets there, or before some six year-old joker with a cannon for an arm nails you in the head with it. Sounds easy enough.

So I'm watching the kids in front of me in the batting order kick and run to first, I notice they all overrun the base, touch the bag and then keep on going a few steps because their momentum carries them past it. Alright. No problem. I got this.

So my turn comes, and I kick the ball as hard as I can—I just bury my size four Keds deep in it—and I'm off full speed down the first base line. I step on the bag and keep sailing past. I was safe, and moved a runner from first all the way to third. I heard cheers from my teammates as I walked back to the bag. One kick and I was the Derek Jeter of the kickball diamond. And I was pretty sure Susie Ellison, the Megan Fox of our first grade class, smiled at me.

Then the next kid comes up, and he drills the ball over the shortstop's head into the outfield. The kid on third heads toward home as I run to second, step on the bag before the outfielder can get the ball in, and keep going a few steps. Same as I did at first base, I overrun second. On my way back to the bag, the second baseman hits me in the chest with the ball. I'm tagged out. The inning is over and the run didn't score. And my teammates are no longer cheering. Instead, they are screaming at me in a Milk-Duds-and-adrenaline-fueled rage. Because, according to them, *everyone* knows first base is the only base you are allowed to overrun.

Everyone but me.

It is stated as fact: I am the biggest idiot ever to play kickball. And, if it were up to them, I would never, ever, be allowed on the field again. There is even talk of banning me from gym class altogether. And Susie Ellison is no longer smiling. (Which pretty much blew my shot at asking her to the prom in eleven years.) But here's what confused me: I wasn't bad at kickball—I could kick hard and run fast, catch a fly ball when it came my way, throw it reasonably well to any base—but obviously I wasn't *good* at it either. I couldn't understand how I could be technically good at something, yet suck so badly at it at the same time. And that's when the epiphany light bulb went on in my head: *The only reason I wasn't good at it, wasn't successful at it, and didn't win when I played was because I didn't know the rules of the game.*

From then on, before I got involved in anything—sports, games, business, writing, dating, cooking, whatever—I made sure to learn all the rules, paying close attention to which ones could be bent, and which ones could be broken. I learned all the strategies and tactics, the ins and the outs any way that I could. Why? Because, I had discovered, that knowing the rules was the secret to success.

You can have all the right tools—athletic ability, intelligence, talent, looks, or connections—but if you don't master the rules of the game, well, my friend, you are screwed. You might as well not even get in the ring. Because a guy who may have a lot less in his tool bag, but possesses a keen understanding of the rule-book—and how to manipulate it—can knock you the fuck out. But I wasn't the first to come to this realization. About 2,500 years before I had my "Ah-ha!" moment on the kickball field, a Chinese general named Sun Tzu had his on the battle field.

While commanding the armies of the Kingdom of Wu in ancient China, Sun Tzu wrote *The Art of War*, arguably the most important book on warfare ever written. At the beginning, he boasts, "The general who hearkens to my counsel and acts upon it will conquer." A pretty ballsy statement, but it ain't bragging if you can back it up. And for nearly 3,000 years, he has. So much so that, for centuries, his little book has been required reading for commanders of armed forces—as well as commanders-in-training at military academies—worldwide. In fact, Sun Tzu's strategies and tactics are so effective that they've also been successfully applied outside of the military, particularly by those looking to crush their opponents in politics and business.

Which brings us to this book you're holding in your hands right now. See, he didn't know it at the time, but Sun Tzu was the original mack daddy. He not only laid out the rules, strategies, and tactics for conquering enemies and winning wars, he also laid out the rules, strategies, and tactics for conquering women and getting laid. Because, as you'll discover, there is little difference between dating women and staging a coup. In fact, everything Sun Tzu taught his generals in *The Art of War* about defeating entire battalions and successfully invading countries, can be used just as effectively by guys who want to meet entire battalions of women and successfully invade a few things of their own.

Think about it. Look at the couples you see every day: Are all the hot girls you see only on the arms of great looking guys? Rich guys? Guys with six-pack abs and twenty-one-inch biceps? Of course not. And I'll bet you and your buddies do the same thing me and my buddies used to do: Point and ask, "What the hell is she doing with him?" before crying in your beer about how you're not good looking enough, rich enough, built enough, tall enough, or even lucky enough to hook up with a chick like that.

But by now that light bulb should be going off, and you should be realizing one simple, important fact: You already have all the tools you need to meet women. You already are *good* at meeting women. The only reason you think you are *bad* at it, and haven't been successful with the women you want to be successful with, has nothing to do with how you look, how much money you have, or how much you can bench press. *It's solely because no one ever taught you the rules of the game.*

Well that's all gonna change. Sun Tzu and I are about to school you in the proven strategies and tactics that you can use in any dating situation. All have been "field tested" by thousands of men who bravely and selflessly marched into the trenches before you, engaging our worthy adversary, then reporting back on what got them shot down, and what ended with "Mission Accomplished." It's priceless intel that many have sacrificed their honor and pride to obtain.

So if you truly want to understand how to be successful with women, read on. Because to paraphrase what Sun Tzu boasted centuries ago, "The gentleman who hearkens to my counsel and acts upon it . . . will score."

CHAPTER 1
LAYING PLANS

"Love and war are the same thing, and stratagems and policy are as allowable in the one as in the other."

—Miguel de Cervantes, author of *Don Quixote*

History's most influential thinkers have built philosophies around it. The greatest writers of our time have devoted books to it. Poets have penned sonnets in honor of it. Hell, Pat Benatar even sang about it.

So if you haven't yet come to the realization that dating is actually a war—a strategic battle of the sexes where the victor truly gets the spoils—let me hit you with some shock and awe: This battle has been raging ever since Eve used her apple as an "Adam Bomb," way back in the Conflict of the Garden of Eden. And make no mistake, women have been winning the war ever since.

This shouldn't come as a surprise. Women are much better prepared than we are. They are far more accomplished at gathering and sharing intel, will cover each other's flanks in a firefight like a tightly knit SEAL team, are naturally adept at deflecting enemy advances, and—as any man who has ever come home at three in the morning smelling of stale whiskey and strange perfume can tell you—their skill at extracting every last shred of information with cunningly relentless interrogation would make even top-level CIA operatives wet their government-issued tighty-whiteys.

They are, in every respect, shrewd and worthy adversaries.

So how can we gain a small foothold in this war and bring home a few victories? By taking Sun-Tzu's first, and most important, piece of counsel before going into any battle: laying plans.

FAIL TO PLAN AND YOU PLAN TO FAIL

By "laying plans" I don't mean what you plan to do once you get her in the bedroom back at your place. (You're getting way ahead of yourself.) I'm talking about getting your plan together *before* you and your buddies head out, so you're not blindly charging onto love's battlefield, stepping on land mines, and getting shot down. Before you suit up and hit the town, you need to have a strategy.

That's right. I said *strategy*. Because as Sun Tzu teaches, "The general who wins a battle makes many calculations in his temple before the battle is fought." And right now, the typical plan of attack for most guys is less General Patton masterfully moving his troops through Europe, kicking ass and taking names (and phone numbers), and more Five-Monkeys-with-a-Gun, recklessly shooting at anything and everything that gets within range. (Tell me that doesn't sound familiar.)

Keep in mind that, after spending years in the trenches deflecting the advances of an endless barrage of jerks, douchebags, and assholes bombarding them with lame pickup lines and awkward approaches, most women have their defenses up. Way before you see them at the bar sipping on Cosmotinis they've already spent hours in the War Room discussing their plan for every aspect of the evening including where they'll go, how long they'll stay, who's gonna drive and not drink, where they'll put their purses while they dance, and The Big One: how they'll handle men who dare try to approach them. They go in with a "No Woman Left Behind" mentality. (Which is chick code for: "No Woman Leaves with a Guy Like You.") So, to get past their Bitch Shields—the mean, nasty, or downright rude things a woman says or does as a main line of defense against approaching men—you're going to need a plan, too. And a good one. The very first thing Sun Tzu teaches us is, "The art of war is governed by five constant factors, all of which need to be taken into account. They are:

- Moral Law
- Heaven
- Earth
- The Commander
- Method and Discipline.

How important are these five factors? I would say they're right up there with air, single malt scotch, and the NFL Network. Sun Tzu himself says, "He who knows them will be victorious; He who knows them not, will fail." So, if you want to take your first steps on the road to victory, read 'em, learn 'em, and live 'em.

Moral Law

When Sun Tzu spoke of "Moral Law," he wasn't talking about the moral code you follow when it comes to dating. *Who* you want to date is entirely up to you. (Personally my moral code includes just three rules: Never date a married woman, never date a friend's ex, and never date a buddy's family member—unless, of course, she's really, really hot.) What Sun Tzu means by Moral Law is that the group needs to be "in complete accord with their ruler"; they need to be willing to follow their leader into battle regardless of the dangers or consequences.

Take a look at the guys you go out with. Are they all out for the same thing as you? Do they want to meet women, or are they already attached and/or miserable, jealous of seeing you hook up with a different girl every weekend? Is there a guy in your group who can't stand to see you talking to a beautiful woman and cockblocks you every chance he gets, butting into your conversation and putting you down in an attempt to get her for himself? I'm sure you roll with at least one of these guys. We all do. Listen, most guys are great friends when it comes to general hanging out, but they can be completely different when it comes to going out to meet women. This doesn't mean they are bad guys or shitty friends or that you should drop them. It just means that on the nights you go out on a mission to meet women, you need to pick your wingmen wisely. (I'll give you the five attributes of a good wingman when I discuss Method and Discipline in a minute.)

You need to make sure everyone agrees to stick to the plan, has the same objectives in mind, and that everyone has each other's back. Because if they don't, everything else you plan for the night will get thrown into a tailspin.

HEAVEN

According to Sun Tzu, Heaven "signifies night and day, cold and heat, times and seasons." All are conditions that need to be taken into careful consideration when planning for any battle. For instance, an army will need different provisions to march in the dead of winter than it will when marching in the heat of summer. Approaching an enemy camp under cover of night requires a much different strategy than a midday attack. A war fought in the thick of the jungle is nothing like one fought in desert sands. So knowing where, when, and what the conditions will be when you approach women will have a big effect on your strategy.

For example, going up to a woman in a club on a Saturday night, when she's expecting to be hit on yet again, requires a very different tactic than approaching a woman who catches your eye in a mall at one in the afternoon. A girl you meet on the beach over the weekend, when she's hanging out in her bikini, will react differently than she would on Monday morning when you see her on the train in her business suit. A woman you stop on the street during a cold, windy, winter day isn't going to be as likely to stand around long, listening to what you have to say as a woman you meet having a glass of wine, enjoying a piece of art in a gallery or museum. (And those, by the way, can be much better places to meet women than a bar. More on that in Chapter 9.) So you have to tailor your approach—and, yes, I'll show you how in later chapters. Keep the where, when, what, and how in mind as you lay out your plans.

EARTH

Earth, according to Sun Tzu, represents "distances great and small; danger and security; open ground and narrow passes; the chances of life and death." Make no mistake; it may not be a matter of life or death, but there *are* dangers when approaching women. And planning for them in advance can mean the difference between heading home with your arm around a hot babe, and heading to the emergency room with some jealous guy's knuckle prints in your jaw.

Quick quiz: There are two chicks you're thinking of approaching in a bar. One is sitting by herself, quietly sipping on her cocktail and glancing around. The other is in a group of about five or six people, both girls and guys, who are laughing and having a great time. Who do you approach?

Most guys would say the one sitting alone at the bar. The other girl is having fun with her friends, and probably isn't into talking to anyone new. Since she came alone, the one sitting by herself looks like she's there to meet a guy, and therefore might be the perfect target. Except she isn't. The only thing you'll gain from going over there is certain embarrassment—or worse.

Remember, as with any good bit of recon, you need to look deeper and be more observant. How many women do you know who are willing to go to a bar or club alone? (Ones that aren't there for "professional reasons," I mean.) Very, very few, if any at all. So it's safe to assume she's waiting for someone. A girlfriend? Maybe. But, in the more common scenario, this woman is waiting for her boyfriend or husband. And chances are, even if she pays attention to you and enters into a conversation, he is most likely going to show up before you can get her number. (If she had any inclination to offer it at all.) And when he finds you talking to his girl, he's probably not going to offer to buy you a drink.

So, now that you have a handle on "Earth" and know the risks, which girl would you approach? Exactly.

THE COMMANDER

"The Commander," doesn't mean the crazy old guy who hangs out in your neighborhood bar wearing vintage British military whites and a handlebar mustache. To Sun Tzu, the Commander "stands for the virtues of wisdom, sincerity, benevolence, courage, and strictness."

Quick story: I have this friend. He's a great guy and hanging with him is always a good time. But he has a friend who he brings out with us once in a while. He's also a great guy, but he's never a good time to hang with because the second the first few drops of alcohol pass his lips, he becomes this raging, loudmouthed, in-your-face asshole who is hell bent on either starting some shit, or driving away the ladies with his antics.

So of course, my buddy never forewarns me that this guy is coming with us because he knows I won't show up if he's there. See, my plan is usually to go out, have a few drinks, have a good time, and meet some women, and this becomes a mission impossible when this other guy is around.

Look at your own group again. Are your wingmen all "Commanders" who are in control under any circumstance, in it to enjoy themselves and score some trophies, or is there one who is looking to blow off a week's worth of aggravation and stress by drinking himself half blind and taking a swing at the bouncer? Remember, it's hard to get a girl's number when you're all sitting in the back alley after being tossed by the "security team." When you're heading out, plan to take only those guys you would want by your side in a real firefight; trust me, your evening will be longer, more fun, and more productive.

METHOD AND DISCIPLINE

Sun Tzu says, "Method and Discipline are to be understood the marshaling of the army in its proper subdivisions, the graduations of rank among the officers." He was a stickler for discipline, and it was important that every single member of his army knew his place in the chain of command.

Very few accomplished pick up artists venture out into the field solo. Like fighter pilots out on patrol, they almost always take a wingman or two with them. And, to use the military jargon the term is borrowed from, they expect their wingmen to stay close, fly straight, and do everything in their power to prevent them from getting shot down.

Does the group of guys you plan to head out with know what it takes to be a good wingman? And I don't mean willingness to throw themselves on a grenade by taking the ugly one so you can be with her hot friend. I'm talking about the *true* rules of being a good wingman that originally appeared in an article my buddy Bobby Rio wrote for TheBachelorGuy.com. There are five, and they are:

INTRODUCE YOUR FRIENDS TO WOMEN

How many times have you been in a bar and seen one guy talking to a chick, while his buddy stands around like an idiot, trying to act like he's enjoying himself all alone? A true wingman invites his buddy into the conversation with a positive introduction that pumps him up a bit: "Have you met my friend John? He has the most interesting job." Don't feel uncomfortable inviting him in. Your buddy is an experienced wingman who knows better than to jack your opportunity with the girl. And introducing him has many benefits. Not only does it make you look better to the girl you're talking to because it shows you are a gentleman and value your friends, but it gives your buddy the opportunity to either meet her friends, or you an excuse to invite another girl into the conversation.

NEVER TALK BAD ABOUT EACH OTHER

Busting balls is part of being a guy. And it's a part we don't want to give up, except when women are around. Good natured ribbing in moderation is fine—and may even get the ladies to drop their guard and join in—but talking smack about something truly personal or embarrassing, like your buddy's chronic body odor problem and the "special" deodorant his doctor prescribed or the fact that he breastfed until he was nine, is off limits. Bringing it up not only embarrasses him, but hurts your chances as well because it makes you look like an insensitive ass. Which leads us to . . .

ALWAYS HAVE YOUR BUDDY'S BACK

The old cliché "Bros before hos" isn't just for high-fiving frat boys. If you're with a group, and the girl you're interested in (or any other girl in the group for that matter), starts giving your friend shit, you back him up. Period. It doesn't matter if she's the hottest chick you've ever seen and she's already agreed to go back to your place and do things to you that are illegal in thirty-seven states—and parts of Canada. He's your boy and you need to defend him at all costs. Someday you might need him to do the same for you.

BLOCK COCKBLOCKERS

There's one in every crowd: the bitter friend who never gets hit on, or is married and miserable, or is just generally jealous of her friends. She's made it her sole mission in life is to make sure her friends don't meet a guy and leave her in the bar, alone. Your job as a good wingman, is to identify the cockblocker (also referred to as "The Grenade," because she has the ability to blow the whole thing to pieces), and keep her occupied while your buddy does his thing. Yeah, I know. Entertaining some drunk, bitchy chick to keep her from torpedoing your friend's chances isn't the most enjoyable way to spend your night out. But tonight it's your job. Tomorrow night it might be his. So be a good soldier, accept your mission, and perform it well.

NEVER FIGHT OVER A GIRL

There are far too many women out there to fight over one with a friend. There's nothing sadder than seeing two guys in a bar trying to outdo and one up each other, all in a feeble attempt to impress some girl. Both usually end up going home alone, looking foolish.

The agreement my friends and I have is simple: The first guy to talk to a girl has the first shot at her. End of story. You do not, under any circumstances, try to steal her from him. Even if you think she could be "The One," you stand down. Only when he decides during the course of the night that he's not interested, does she become fair game.

So take another look at the guys you are planning to roll with. Do you think they can enjoy a night out while following the rules of a good wingman? Because understand this, even if you don't come out and say, "Hey Ralph, you're my wingman tonight, okay buddy?" he will be just that since he's going to be barhopping and chasing chicks with you all night. Like it or not, anything and everything he says or does will have an effect on your success.

For example: If Ralph makes an ass of himself while you're talking to a group of people by asking the girls to "let their sweater puppies come out and play"; or if you're having a great time talking to a beautiful woman and he runs over and throws up on her friend's shoes after spending the last hour and a half doing Jäger Bombs at the bar with a bunch of frat boys on Spring Break; or if you introduce him to a girl you've been talking to for a while, and he looks at her chest and inexplicably starts to shake his head violently and make motorboat sounds . . . it's Game Over. I know because I've had all of those things happen to me and they brought an abrupt end to otherwise successful campaigns; snatched defeat right from the jaws of victory. Might as well hoist up the white flag and retreat back home before you sustain any more casualties.

ASK QUESTIONS

Now you can understand why the Five Factors were so important to Sun Tzu, and why they were the foundation of every plan he laid before he even raised his sword. And while laying out those plans and choosing generals to lead his men into battle, he would ask himself several questions first. Questions, he said, that allowed him "to forecast victory or defeat" with extreme certainty before even setting foot on the battlefield. Here's how to adapt and use Sun Tzu's questions when laying your own plans, deciding what type of attack you're going to use, and choosing which "generals" will ride into battle with you:

WHICH IS IMBUED WITH THE MORAL LAW?

When deciding who you're going to roll with for the night, you first need to make the goal of the night clear. Then ask yourself which of your friends understands your goals and agrees with them. Keep in mind that not every guy is up for a night of chasing ass and taking phone numbers. Those that are already attached may be uncomfortable heading out with a bunch of guys who plan on bouncing from bar to bar looking to score. This type of guy may be miserable all night, become an anchor around your neck, and drag you down with him. Then there is the aforementioned alcohol-induced instant-asshole whose idea of a great night out is waking up in county lock-up with dried blood running from his nose, a court appointed lawyer, and you as his cellmate. So when laying plans, ask yourself: Are we going to hang with the guys and watch the game at a sports bar, or suit up and hit the clubs looking for women? Then decide who the right "generals" are for that particular plan.

WHICH OF THEM HAS THE MOST ABILITY?

So you've decided it's a night for wild women and wingmen. Naturally, some of your friends are going to be better at handling themselves in this type of social situation than others—and those are the ones you are going to want to have by your side. Now that doesn't mean Steve gets left off the invite list just because he has a tendency to get nervous and stutter around certain women with oversized implants wearing high heels and bright red lipstick. I'm all for having your boy's back and helping him improve his skills. It just means you want to plan ahead; make sure you've got a strong wingman along with you to have your back in case you need it.

WITH WHOM LIE THE ADVANTAGES DERIVED FROM HEAVEN AND EARTH?

Who will you be "targeting?" When's the time and what's the place of your mission? Will you be at an advantage or disadvantage there? Take this into serious consideration when planning. Are you and the guys headed to the beach or the club? What about a steakhouse for dinner? Remember that women flying solo can be dangerous targets, but women are more apt to go to the beach alone, than to a bar or club. So, if you're at the beach and you see a solo target, approaching her may be less risky and let you launch into your rap without worrying about cockblockers, grenades, or overprotective friends, giving you an advantage.

If you're at the club, it can be easy for you to enter a group of people and talk to everyone, increasing your odds—and adding to your advantage. However, if you're at a steakhouse and think the hostess is flirting with you, be careful. She may be up there alone and present an attractive target, but—and this may come as a shock to some of you—she's a hired gun and is paid to flirt with you. (As are other "hired guns" like bartenders, waitresses, and strippers.) In this case, *she* has the distinct advantage. You're on her home turf, and she has a million excuses as to why she can't give you her number. I'm not saying a pick up is impossible, but it will take a different plan and approach. Sun Tzu took all of this into account. You should too, so tailor your plans accordingly.

ON WHICH SIDE IS THE DISCIPLINE THE MOST RIGOROUSLY ENFORCED?

There are definitely times when getting sloppy is not only appropriate, it's entirely called for: during bachelor parties, after a bad break up, any time your team loses a close Game 7, and the day Emmanuelle Chriqui gets married. But when your mission is to meet women? Not one of those times. You need to have your wits about you. Let's take a look at the Advantage/Disadvantage Chart for Drunk Pickups:

You're Sober **She's Sober** Advantage—Push	In this situation, success will come down to factors like attraction and comfort. And it's the best way to meet a woman if you plan on dating her for a while.
You're Sober **She's Drunk** Advantage—You. Mostly	Sure it's easier to get a chick into a conversation when she's drunk, and she'll laugh at just about anything. And, depending on her blood alcohol level, she'll agree to just about anything too. But is that the game you're after? It's like shooting animals in the zoo and calling yourself a hunter.
You're Drunk **She's Drunk** Advantage—You. Mostly	This is one of those, grab-the-popcorn-and-let-the-comedy-begin situations. Anything can happen, and it usually does. Remember college? And what you used to wake up next to? Yeah, let's try to keep that in the past.
You're Drunk **She's Sober** Advantage—Her	The last thing you want to do is give her any more advantages than she already has. You want to succeed? Stay sharp, stay focused, and, if the alcohol starts to take hold and you find yourself starting to say or do stupid things, treat it like the drive home: Hand the keys to your wingman and let him take the wheel. Your new mission is to sit and smile and not fuck anything up.

Now that you have a plan that takes the Five Factors into account, made sure everyone is on board, have asked and answered the Four Questions and concluded victory is obtainable, and selected the right "generals" who will do whatever it takes to make the mission a success, you need to take a look in the mirror. Because before you fly your wingmen into enemy territory, you need to ask yourself: Are you prepared to lead this mission?

At the end of every chapter, there will be a "Post-Training Debriefing" where you'll get a quick bullet point debriefing of all the important points you need to take away.

- Dating is actually a war, a strategic battle of the sexes. And women are kicking our asses. Why? Because they've been deflecting the advances of jerks and douchebags for years, they're better prepared for battle, and they have a better game plan that includes a "No Woman Gets Left Behind" mentality.
- If you want to win the battle, and your goal for the night is to meet women, you're going to need a game plan with a strategy of your own. Your best strategy should be governed by Sun Tzu's Five Constant Factors:

  - **Moral Law:** Everyone you roll with has the same goal in mind, has your back all night, and agrees to stick to the plan.
  - **Heaven:** Keep the where, when, what, and how in mind as you lay out your plans.
  - **Earth:** Understand the risks in approaching women, what to look out for, and how to avoid traps.
  - **The Commander:** Take only those wingmen you'd want by your side in a real firefight, guys we'll call Commanders, not the joker who wants to get shitfaced and roll around in the alley with the bouncers.
  - **Method and Discipline:** Make sure your wingmen understand and follow the five rules of being wingmen.

- If your goal for the night is to go out and meet women, ask yourself Sun Tzu's critical questions when choosing which generals are going to ride into battle with you.
- When partaking of adult beverages, remember the Advantage/Disadvantage Chart for Drunk Pickups.

CHAPTER 2

ON WAGING WAR

"It is as a soldier that you make love and as a lover that you make war."
—Antione de Saint-Expury, author of *The Little Prince*

Do you know the real purpose of putting a military recruit through boot camp? Besides giving him the "high and tight" hair cut and making olive drab his new favorite color? According to military historian Gwynn Dyer, boot camp training (or recruit training as it's officially known), is "the process of transforming civilians into soldiers, sailors, coast guardsmen, marines, or airmen as a form of conditioning in which inductees are encouraged to partially submerge their individuality for the good of their unit. . . . This conditioning is essential for military function because combat requires people to endure stress and perform actions which are simply not present in normal life."

Interesting. Personally, I always thought the point of boot camp was to get raw recruits physically ready for combat—teach them to shoot and drive tanks, and get them conditioned to hike long distances—but it turns out that one of the major goals of the training is to get them *psychologically* ready for combat. This makes perfect sense; you'd want to know as soon as possible if a guy could take the pressure of being under fire, before he has a Private Pyle–like meltdown and puts his platoon's lives at risk.

Consider this chapter the boot camp of your dating training. You're going to find out the kind of guy you need to be—both mentally and personality-wise—to truly be successful with women, to overcome some of the most common fears and anxieties, and to mold yourself into the perfect general to lead your men into battle and engage targets. Where, to paraphrase Mr. Dyer, you will definitely endure stress (of talking to strangers and facing possible rejection), and perform actions (like approaching multiple groups of very attractive women), that are simply not present in your normal life.

SCHOOL YOURSELF

When Sun Tzu wrote *The Art of War*, he didn't do it to teach those who read it how to fire a weapon, build bombs, or interrogate prisoners. He wrote it as a broad overview of the most important principles of war: to teach those who read it how to achieve complete and undeniable victory over any opponent with tested, proven, and masterful strategies and tactics. He wanted his generals to be men of honor, men who were willing to mold themselves into generals who could go into any battle and win, not soldiers who relied on dirty tricks or gimmicks. Warriors thoroughly schooled in the art of war, not men who learned just enough to fake their way through a few battles.

It's the same when it comes to dating, so let me get real for a minute. This book is not about "getting over" on women or tricking them into bed or any other kind of similar assorted douchebaggery. If that's what you're looking for, I suggest you stop reading now. Put the book back on the shelf and spend the money on an Ed Hardy t-shirt or face bronzer instead. This isn't for you.

Any moron can throw out some canned opening lines, pretend to be something he's not for a night, and talk a chick into bed once in a while. Those are the chuckleheads the term "getting lucky" was created for, because for them it was luck—that and just plain playing the odds. After all, if you approach a couple hundred women, one or two are bound to fall for that bullshit. But this is about learning the skills necessary to become a real warrior in the battle of the sexes, a man women truly want to meet. And date. And play sheet hockey with. Because you're not going to be able to keep up a charade long term when you do finally meet that one you want to stay with for a while; we both know that she'll eventually see through to the "real you" and bail. No, this is about learning what you have to do to attract women to you—and keep them attracted.

So, are you prepared? And do you understand what it's going to take to accomplish your mission of succeeding with women? Are you ready to make changes, even if it means ditching some of your current behaviors and habits—and adopting new ones? Can you change your personal style, overcome some fears and preconceived notions about yourself, and become a man women are irresistibly attracted to? Because, my friends, that is what it takes to succeed with women.

WHAT WOMEN WANT, ISN'T WHAT THEY REALLY WANT

Raise your hand if you've ever been forced to take one of those relationship quizzes they put in women's magazines to make our lives miserable. You know the ones I'm talking about. They ask her what she wants in a relationship, and then ask her to ask you what you're looking for in a relationship. Then you break up a week later because you scored "Ditch Him, Girl" on your compatibility score, instead of "Put a Ring on It."

So quiz veterans, what's the number one thing women always say they find attractive in men? If you said "sense of humor" award yourself ten points. That's what the majority of women say when asked what they look for in a guy. Try it one day. Take an informal poll of women you know, and ask them what they look for. You'll also get things like "caring and sensitive," "must love dogs," "listens to what I have to say," or even "has to be taller than me." Every once in a while you'll even hear the occasional honest answer like "rich, 'cause I ain't working no more." But I guarantee "sense of humor" will be one of the first one or two answers the majority of your female poll-ees will give you.

So how come all the hot chicks aren't dating 6-foot-2 stand-up comedians who cry at sad movies and tell jokes with a dog on stage? The answer is simple: What women *tell* you they want in a guy *isn't really what they want in a guy.* Let me clarify. What they tell you may very well be what they *want* in a guy, but it isn't what ultimately *attracts* them to a guy. Huge difference.

And if you need proof, just think of all the great girls you know who complain that they desperately want to find a nice, caring guy who'll treat them well, open doors for them, take them to romantic dinners, and curl up on the couch on a Saturday night watching chick flicks and giving foot massages and yet always seem to date assholes, self-centered jerks, and bad boys. And this goes on while you, and every other Average Frustrated Chump (AFC) out there, provide a shoulder to cry on and a willing ear to listen. Then you go home alone with a pounding headache and mascara smudges on your shirt.

So are they lying to us? Using this as some sort of battlefield deception to confuse us and throw us off balance. I don't think so. I think the truth is that they really don't understand that what they want in a guy and what they are actually attracted to are two completely different things. (Which is also why, in my humble opinion, women don't write effective dating books for men. They write page after page about how we should be to get and keep women based on what they *think* they want, versus what actually works on them.)

The good news is, you're about to find out what really attracts women the most. The better news? It will give you a distinct advantage when you and your wingmen engage your "targets."

PUT ME IN COACH

A while back, while researching an article for a magazine, I was invited to sit in on a dating class for men. Two "dating coaches," who spent three days schooling twelve to fifteen guys in the art of meeting women, taught the class. Part of the course included two nights of "in the field" training at local nightspots, where they pushed and prodded these guys to put the strategies and tactics they learned in the classroom each day to work in a practical situation by trying them on actual women each night. Then they critiqued their results, offered advice on how to improve, and turned them loose into the crowd again. Sometimes they literally pushed these guys into "sets" (the term for the groups of people you engage with, the "target" being the girl you are ultimately after), if they were too reluctant—or too scared—to get back out there and face rejection again. It was perfect "theory into practice" training and it's the same way young, untrained men are molded into soldiers in boot camps.

Now, you're probably thinking that it sounds like I'm talking about pick up artists. And you would be right, because that's exactly what those guys were. Only they prefer to be called dating coaches, which, when you're charging $2,000–$3,000 per weekend per person for the class, sounds a lot more profes-sional. Like you probably do right now, I had a preconceived notion before I went into the class. I fully expected it would be filled with losers, geeks, parent's basement dwellers, forty-year-old virgins, and other assorted members of the Desperate and Dateless, who were willing to pay a ridiculously exorbitant fee just to learn how to get laid. I also figured the class would be taught by guys who were conniving misogynists out to provide their eager trainees with volumes of deception and chicanery they could use to fool women into sleeping with them. I already had the article's angle thought out before I went in: It was going to be a snarky humor piece where we could all laugh together at the exploits of the lonely losers, and mock the preening ego-maniacs who mentored them, while pulling back the curtain on their tricks and cons.

Except that's not how the class was at all. Rather than being filled with guys who spoke Klingon and looked like extras from *The Big Bang Theory*, they were a fairly representative cross sec-tion of guys everywhere. There were young, recent college grads who wanted to improve their social skills, guys who did okay with women but wanted to do a lot better, and middle aged, recently divorced professionals who hadn't been on a date in over twenty years and wanted to know what to do now that they were back in the game. No one you'd really have the urge to give a wedgie to after gym class.

And the instructors were a couple of guys you'd actually like to have a beer or two with. Far from looking like over-groomed, overly toned Abercrombie and Fitch models or behaving like over-bearing cavemen constantly bragging about their sexual exploits, they were average-looking guys who were entertaining, engaging, and told some very interesting stories. They were guys you'd be comfortable hanging out with, which is their whole point. The way to build attraction goes way beyond the physical and starts with being all of those things I just mentioned: being the kind of guy a girl is comfortable with, enjoys spending time with, and really wants to be around.

ENTERTAINING? YES. DANCING MONKEY? NO.

Think about when you go out. If you had the choice between hanging with a buddy who tells great stories, starts conversations with everyone who walks by, and is generally piss-yourself funny all night long and a buddy who likes to stand in a corner all night, drinking beer and only getting excited when he successfully peels the label off his beer bottle in one piece, which would you choose? Unless you're going through an emo phase, you're choosing Buddy Number One 99.999 percent of the time. Because fun and interesting, trumps boring and dull every time.

Do you think it's any different for women? Do you think given the choice between an average-looking guy who is entertaining, engaging, exciting, and fun to be around and some good looking mope standing in a corner, brooding, and staring at chicks across the bar, that she'd choose to walk over and start talking to Mopey? Of course not. And here's the news flash if you haven't figured it out already: She's out to have a good time too. Probably even more so than you.

While your mission may be to hit the bars, find chicks, and try to hook up, her mission (for the most part) is to go out with a bunch of friends, have some drinks, maybe dance a little, and have fun. Hooking up enters her mind only if she finds a guy who attracts her enough. So, instead of planning to go out, seek targets, and get laid, make it your new mission to be that guy who shows her the good time she's looking for. That guy is fun, interesting, exciting, and, above all, entertaining.

But here's an important thing to keep in mind: There's a fine line between being *entertaining*, and being an *entertainer*. When you're entertaining, you're in control of the group; you're telling stories, leading the conversation and making them beg for more. When you're an entertainer, the group is in control of you. You're their jester, their dancing monkey who spends the night begging for their approval. See the difference? In one you're in control, while in the other you're being controlled. One is a position of strength, the other a position of weakness—and women prey on weakness.

So how can you tell when you've crossed over from being entertaining to being an entertainer? It's a subtle difference, but there are signs. For example:

You're entertaining if . . .	You're an entertainer if . . .
. . . you say something like, "Did you know that only 4 percent of the population can form a W with their tongue?" then ask everyone in the group to try, you all laugh as each of them makes an attempt, and you show them that you can do it.	. . . you feel the need to say "Hey watch this!" or "Guess what I can do?!" before performing some ridiculous stunt or Stupid Human Trick.
. . . you're telling interesting stories, and the group is leaning in to listen or asking you to tell another.	. . . you're firing off silly jokes, and they seem to be laughing more at you than with you.
. . . you say you want to show her a couple of old-school break dance moves you picked up while at a club in LA, take her to the dance floor, bust out a couple of ill-performed moves, and she laughs and tries her own moves along with you.	. . . she asks you to "do that thing you were doing before" and laughs at you when you do whatever it was. Here, you're not just an entertainer, you're her personal Dancing Monkey—and I don't have to tell you that Dancing Monkeys don't get laid.

One important thing that I want you to remember is that this process isn't just about changing yourself into the kind of man women want to date. It's about changing yourself into the kind of man *you* want to be. Here's a newsflash for you: High school is over. There are no more cliques. No more social caste systems to keep you down. And no more being labeled a geek, mathlete, burn out, emo, gamer, or anything else that kept you from getting the women you wanted. *The guy you were yesterday is gone.* Stop carrying around that image of yourself as "bad with women." As of right now, you're starting all over from scratch and can be any guy you've ever dreamt of being. But this will only happen if you put the work in and make a conscious effort to change.

The good news is that you get to try on as many "Personality Suits" as you want to see which one fits you best. Which man you choose to present will depend on the following three things:

1. **Who you see yourself as:** Are you the suave Don Draper type? The indie rock hipster? The sensitive artist? The wise-cracking, self-assured Barney Stinson, suited up and ready to roll? See which fits your style and personality best. As paradoxical as it sounds, you want to be "yourself." Someone you can be comfortable being.

2. **What social group you want to be associated with:** Think of the people you are going to associate yourself with as your "battalion." If you see yourself as the indie hipster, you'd better love the music and culture associated with it.

3. **What kind of woman you want to attract:** If you have a thing for tree-hugging, free-loving hippie chicks, then being the Don Draper type, wearing designer suits, and chatting about international affairs, probably won't work. Opposites attract? That's romantic horseshit. Women tend to go for guys they can relate to.

Keep in mind, the next babe you approach has no idea you were a *Dungeons and Dragons* geek or a comic book fanboy back in college. She won't know you spent most of your life so shy and afraid to talk to anyone that you spent most Saturday nights on the couch watching *Dr. Who* marathons, or that your graduating class voted you Most Likely to Die a Virgin. That's all in the past. It's over. This is the first inning of a whole new ball game. That's what we're going to work on from here on out, so give yourself permission to have a fresh start.

And that's about as touchy-feely as I'm going to get. Almost turned the corner into Oprah territory there. I'm gonna have to go pour myself a shot of single malt, light a cigar, and hit the massage parlor to shake that off.

WAR STORY: You Can Either Go to the Party . . . Or You Can Be the Party

Here's the set up: Twenty of us pile into a party bus and head for South Beach for a bachelor party. The minute we hit the first club, one guy, Connor, is off the bus and into the crowd. Now Connor is a fairly quiet guy, mostly unassuming. Not a guy that you would say is classically good-looking. Yet he is dancing with any chick that gets close. Tall ones, fat ones, older ones, hot ones . . . doesn't matter because Connor can't really dance. Regardless, he is pulling women onto the dance floor and throwing together a collection of moves right out of a bad '80s dance movie. Not being a Dancing Monkey and acting foolish for the enjoyment of others, but having a great time himself and making sure the girls around him are too.

The rest of us are either watching him or getting dragged out onto the dance floor with him and whatever group of girls he's with at the time. Either way, we are all laughing our asses off. So are the people around us, many of whom are chicks asking who he is, who *we* are, and what we are doing there that night. Boom. Instant ice breaker. Thanks to Connor, we are now in conversations with women. Hot women.

Connor is collecting phone numbers left and right from the women he's danced with who want to know when he'll be back at the club. And a lot of these women are gorgeous. Seriously gorgeous. (If you know anything about South Beach, you know the place is swarming with models.) Women who, had they seen him on the street, or if he'd walked up and said hi, wouldn't have given him a second look. But he was fun, he was the center of attention, and he made their night memorable. They gave him their numbers because they wanted to have that incredibly fun experience again and they knew he was the guy who knew could give it to them. Even the rest of us were getting, "Call me next time you guys come to South Beach. Here's my number" a lot. His popularity had extended to us simply because we were with him. (Remember the Five Factors from Chapter 1? Connor was the perfect General to go into battle with.)

But here's the important takeaway from this story: When we got back on the bus after that first stop, I asked Connor where that all came from. I mean, he's never shown signs of that kind of personality before. And he told me that years ago when he was a shy freshman in college who was having trouble meeting women and basically just standing around at parties, he had an upper classman give him some advice: "You have a choice. You can either go to the party. Or you can be the party."

GRAB ANXIETY BY THE THROAT

So, again, Mission One is to forget that your intention is to "pick up" women. Forget that you haven't gotten laid since Pluto was a planet. Take that pressure off yourself. Instead, relax and enjoy yourself. Focus on having energy. Have fun. Be exciting. Smile. Talk to people. Be interesting and engaging. Be the guy people want to be around. Just have a great time, and the women you approach will too.

Yeah, I know that's easier said than done. How is it possible to relax and have a great time when you're sweating like Roger Clemens in front of the grand jury? Simple. Practice. See, one of the main reasons most guys get nervous going up and starting a conversation with a woman they're attracted to—what some dating coaches call "Approach Anxiety"—is because they're attracted to her. So part of your boot camp training is to condition yourself to think of approaching hot women as no big deal, or even as something enjoyable. This comes down to nothing but your mindset.

Think of it like this: If you were in a store buying shoes and the salesperson was a middle-aged, overweight woman in an ill-fitting, polyester suit, with dandruff flakes in her hair, and a makeup job that made her look like a weekend drag queen, would you be nervous talking to her? Of course not. Because you're not attracted to her. You could walk right up, ask her for the shoes, make an offhanded comment about her suit, and maybe even suggest a new shampoo—all without breaking a sweat. But if the salesperson was a young blond wearing a red leather mini with matching fuck-me pumps, legs that went on for miles, and a top that barely kept her ample assets from popping out into public view, you might get sweaty palms at the thought of asking her for those size 11 black wingtips even though it's just a business transaction.

And that's normal. Every guy goes through it. It's a mental block that comes from years of fearing rejection from women— or years of suffering *actual* rejection from women—and maybe even from some shyness and a general fear of talking to people you don't know. But that doesn't mean you have to suffer from it for the rest of your life. There are ways to get over it. In fact, one of my dating coach buddies, Carlos Xuma, wrote a great short e-book called *The Approach Anxiety Annihilator*. (You can grab a free copy for yourself at *www.DatingDynamics.com.*) In it he explains one of the best ways to overcome approach anxiety, "The Hit & Run 50." He calls it his "gold nugget," of approach advice, and all you have to do is simply approach fifty random women and pay each one a sincere compliment. It doesn't matter how long it takes you. Some guys might be able to hit up fifty women in a week, some might take a month or longer. But the key is to merely walk up to fifty women you don't know—preferably women you are not attracted to so there's no underlying intention of trying to turn it into a pick up—and just give them a compliment.

Try saying something like, "Wow, those are really cool sunglasses, they really fit your face well" or "I don't mean to interrupt, but I just had to let you know you have the best smile I've seen in a long time." Then simply turn and walk away. Don't wait for validation or for her to think you're trying to hit on her. Don't ask for phone numbers, email addresses, or to go grab some coffee. Don't expect anything in return. Just hit and run. You'll definitely make her day—especially if she's not the type that men usually walk up and talk to—and you'll be spreading some joy. She doesn't have to know you had a selfish reason for the compliment.

From Carlos's experience, most guys find that walking up to women stops being weird and awkward and scary way before they hit fifty. And, as the approach anxiety starts to fade away, something else very useful happens: When you talk to strange women and leave them with a smile, that becomes part of your mindset.

You become a guy who makes chicks happier just by having talked to them. And, as Carlos says in his book, "Approaching becomes fun again, when you stop needing a certain outcome from it." (That "certain outcome" being that she agrees to jump into bed with you.) All of this goes back to my earlier point that, when you stop putting the pressure on yourself to constantly pick up, pick up, pick up, and make it more about having fun first, your results will be dramatically different. To give you a quick example of how being relaxed, not looking for the hook up, and just trying to have fun trumps all else, I'll show you how it can even work with women who don't speak the same language as you.

AN INTERNATIONAL AFFAIR. OR TWO.

I was in Mexico recently, as the guest of a certain very large tequila company owned by a guy named Jose, for a huge release party. About a dozen people were invited. Our first night there, the reps running the event took us out to a club—it was called "Mala Noche," or Bad Night in Spanish, so we had high expectations—and several very attractive women showed up who were friends of the local reps. None of them spoke English, and none of us spoke Spanish. Pretty much after the basic "como estas?" we learned in high school, we were screwed. At first there was a lot of smiling and nodding. Then there was just uncomfortable silence.

So I decide to walk over and sit down next to two of the girls who have, by this time, given up on the group thing and are talking only to each other. And I just start talking. Even though I know they have no clue what the hell I'm saying. I smile big, hold my drink up to clink glasses, introduce myself, and tell them that I want them to teach me Spanish so we can talk. Turns out, one knows a little English and got the gist of what I said. So, fueled by mutual interest in each other's languages, and copious amounts of tequila, we start giving each other words and phrases we want to know how to say. And because we have no real way to describe the words or phrases in a way the other person can understand, the whole thing turns into a nightlong game of really bad but really, really funny Drunk International Charades. (Try and act out "sponge bath" without talking after a couple bottles of tequila, and you'll see what I mean.) It started out innocently enough, but by the end of the night, the game had devolved into Drunk International Dirty Words Charades. The night ended with both of them giving me their phone numbers, email addresses, and an invitation to join them at their place the following night. All that and I said essentially nothing substantial the entire time; I just had fun and was entertaining.

If you think you need clever pick up lines and other gimmicks or need to be Brad Pitt's better looking younger brother to meet women, get that out of your head right now. I'll say it again, because it can't be said enough: Start by being the center of attention, being exciting, having a great time, and being the party.

So, congratulations, you've made it through boot camp. Now that you've earned your ribbon, and have your head in the right place to start meeting women, it's time to load up on some of the ammunition you'll need. Read on to discover what kind of fuel you'll use to get her attraction engine running at full bore—and have her thinking of you as bedroom material—before she has a chance to get her defenses in gear. Trust me, you're going to discover the secret to being "attractive," even if you look like Urkel.

- Prepare mentally to be successful with women, and mold yourself into the kind of guy they find attractive. If you want to build attraction, then be "attractive"; i.e., entertaining, exciting, engaging, and fun.
- This process isn't about "getting over" on women, tricking them into bed, or other assorted douchebaggery. It's about learning the skills and traits necessary to become irresistible to women and attract them to you.
- Understand that what women *think* they want in a guy, isn't really what attracts them to a guy.
- Be entertaining, but don't cross over into being an entertainer. One is a position of strength, the other a position of weakness. One you are in control, the other you're being controlled. Like a dancing monkey. And dancing monkeys don't get laid.
- High school is over, and so is whatever clique you were a part of. Women have no idea who you were yesterday. You have the ability to reinvent yourself into the man you want to be.
- You can *go* to the party, or you can *be* the party.
- Everyone's got "Approach Anxiety." Overcome it using the Hit & Run 50 technique.

CHAPTER 3
THE SHEATHED SWORD

"We owe to the Middle Ages the two worst inventions of humanity—romantic love and gunpowder."
—Andre Maurois

This is not a chapter preaching the virtues of safe sex or an instructional guide on how to put on a condom. (Although, if you're going to use this information to score yourself a number of "trophies," you should already get that safe sex is a necessity. No soldier is any good with a damaged weapon.) Rather, "The Sheathed Sword" stratagem concerns the ability to win wars *without ever having to draw a sword.* Sun Tzu wanted his generals to understand that "to fight and conquer in all your battles is not supreme excellence; supreme excellence consists in breaking the enemy's resistance without fighting. . . . Thus, the highest form of generalship is to balk the enemy's plans."

And that's exactly what you want to do when engaging your targets. Remember, women are wily veterans of this war. They enter most social situations with their guard already up, ready to launch a counterstrike at any guy looking to make a move. We've all seen it before: Even an innocent "Hi, my name is . . ." can end with some poor fool shot down before he even has a chance to get off the deck. It would be so much easier to win her over without

33

having to "unsheathe your sword." (Which, if all goes well, you'll end up doing back at your place later.)

So how can you sneak past her Bitch Shield and go from just being another chump in the crowd to someone who asks her how she takes her morning coffee? Simple: You get her to want you, to see you as incredibly desirable. So much so, that she not only drops her defenses, but actually pursues you.

There are a number of characteristics men have that can fuel women's attraction engines—and I'm not talking about looks, six-pack abs, or wallet size. And out of all the characteristics that really get women interested, there are three that top all the others. Not just because they are effective at building attraction, but because they're easy to emulate, don't require a complete personality overhaul, and can be put into play immediately. So keep the following attributes in mind, and be sure to embody them when you step out into the field because they'll get her to drop her guard faster than she dropped her panties on Prom Night.

STRENGTH

I'm not talking about how much you can bench. (Which, honestly, only impresses NFL scouts. And that guy at the gym still wearing spandex shorts.) I'm talking about three very specific types of strength that you can use to make that woman at the bar want you: Mental Strength, Social Strength, and Strength of Character.

MENTAL STRENGTH

We've already briefly gone over this one, but when you flex your metal muscles, you gain the ability to be engaging, exciting, interesting, and entertaining. Great looks may get you get a date or two, but guys who are as sharp as hot butter won't be kept around long. Most women need mental stimulation just as much, if not more, than they need physical stimulation. If you can get her mental juices flowing—and depending on the girl you're targeting, you can do that with humor, fascinating stories, a debate over which indie bands have "sold out" to the establishment, or in-depth discussions of the effects of the socio-political structure on the ever-shrinking middle class—you can look like Pee Wee Herman and she'll think you're the hottest guy in the room.

For proof, look to the romance novels that are basically porn for chicks. If women didn't crave mental stimulation, these books would be about seven or eight pages long; Page 1: They met on a train. Pages 2–7: They had sex. Page 8: She reluctantly went back to her asshole husband. The End. But instead, they're packed with hundreds of pages of descriptive imagery, endless romantic dialog, and every infinitesimal detail you can imagine. We guys don't need as much mental stimulation, which is why the only real plot in our porn is: A couple of hot co-eds ordered a sausage pizza. But women do, and it's a big part of the reason why women love guys who are great storytellers. (I'll get into how you can become a pro at laying down stories later in Chapter 6.)

SOCIAL STRENGTH

Social strength is incredibly powerful; in fact, it's one of the strongest ways to attract a woman. When you have social strength, you command attention from everyone—even other guys. You're the Alpha Male in control of the room, directing the conversation and making everyone laugh. By going from group to group and talking to different women, you build your "social proof" to other people in the room. Women see other women talking to you and having a great time with you and they figure there must be some reason why you're popular with everyone there. They want to know you, and you immediately become more desirable—much more than the guy hanging out in a corner talking only with his buddies or that dude at the bar all alone, staring into his Jack and coke.

Sun Tzu makes a point to say, "The captured soldiers should be kindly treated and kept. This is called using the conquered foe to augment one's own strength." You need to do the same thing to augment your social strength. Face it: You're not going to go home with every woman you meet. You're not going to be attracted to every woman you meet either. Does this mean that, when you realize there's no chance of a little slap and tickle, you cast her aside or make some insulting comment as you strut off? Only if you're a douchebag. Ol' Sun Tzu didn't abide by this, and neither should you. Instead, she can help to augment your social strength.

Because when a chick sees that another chick (or two) is talking to you and having a great time, she starts thinking "Who is this guy? I need to know him." Just like a kid with a toy, when she sees someone else having fun with you, she's gonna want to play with you too. And guess who benefits?

STRENGTH OF CHARACTER

Strength of character is having self-confidence, strength of mind, backbone, and what some might call "swagger." It's also the trickiest characteristic for some guys to keep up. Why? Because this is the one that women will attack and test and chip away at and try to expose. And they'll do this by using a Shit Test: where she'll say or do something intentionally shitty to you for the sole purpose of seeing how you react. In their Love Is War Arsenal, this is their bunker buster. It blasts through any weak walls and burrows down deep, blowing up any chance you've got with her.

And Nice Guys—I'm talking to you right now—this is exactly why you get shit on, again and again and again and again. The women you're with don't want a guy who will roll over, show his belly, and do whatever they say. They crave a guy who is confident, self-assured, and has a mind of his own—and the strength of character to tell them to go fuck themselves if and when the situation warrants. This is not to say you should be a dick, but it means that fawning all over a girl, doing her bidding, buying her drinks, and agreeing with everything she says because you think it will make her "like" you, is dead wrong—and the quickest way to fail her Shit Test.

If you're pushing too hard to get her to like you, not only is she going to think you're a complete pussy (and rightfully so), but she's also going to know immediately that you're trying to get into her pants. All those women in the trenches learned very quickly that the majority of guys use "Nice" as a way to wrangle an invitation to ride the fornication train. Think of Nice as the "So, what's your sign?" pickup technique of today—only not nearly as effective.

Understand that a woman is going to be Shit Testing you all night, looking to see how you react. It's ingrained in her mental wiring as part of her innate survival mechanism. Some of it will be obvious ("Seriously, who picked out *that* shirt for you?" or "Buy me a drink."), some of it so subtle you may miss it ("Can you watch our purses while we dance?"), but she'll be flinging it at you all night from behind her Bitch Shield. The more you let it stick to you, the less chance you have of scoring. So showing her you've got strong character—not being afraid of speaking your mind, having a dissenting opinion, or telling her she's being a bitch when she's being a bitch—will allow you to fend off the relentless barrage of Shit Tests, and get you a lot farther than tucking your dick between your legs and "yes, dear-ing" her all night.

Not sure if you're falling into the sap trap by showing weak character? Here are a few quick tests to tell if you might be a Nice Guy:

YOU MIGHT BE A NICE GUY IF . . .

❏ She says "I'd love another drink," and you push your way through the crowd to buy her another appletini, rather than ask her to grab you a cold one since she's going anyway.

❏ You ask her what kind of music she likes, and she answers "I don't listen to music" in a snippy tone, and you reply "Yeah, I don't either. Music's overrated," instead of something like "You don't listen to music?! What kind of boring, vapid person doesn't listen to music? Are you a Quaker?"

❏ You spend more than two minutes listening to her whine about how her ex dumped her for "that whore," and agree in any way that all men are dogs, pigs, or any other animal-like metaphor in an effort to distance yourself from your brothers.

❏ You tell her that you don't watch sports, just so she won't think you'll be spending weekends on the couch in front of the flat screen instead of taking her antiquing—on the outside chance she agrees to date you.

❏ She displays any kind of rude or obnoxious behavior, and you don't call her out because you think doing so will ruin your chances of getting laid.

❏ You've known her less than an hour and you're already agreeing to help her with anything that requires you to 1. Lift heavy things, 2. Open your wallet, 3. Possibly have to take a punch.

Now, I'm going to get into detail on this when I discuss Qualifying in Chapter 6, but for now, understand that this is why some
guys like to employ a technique called a "Neg," popularized by
legendary pick up artist, Mystery, star of VH1's *The Pickup Artist*,
and subject of Neil Strauss's book *The Game*. It's a little controver-
sial and has gotten a bad rap in some circles, mostly because some
guys have taken it a little too far, but basically it's just a gentle or
playful insult directed to a girl, particularly if she's really hot, say
a 9 or 10. A Neg is something like, "I think it's adorable how your
nostrils flare out when you laugh" or "It takes a pretty confident
woman to pull off a dress like that." You would use a Neg to show
her you're not intimidated or impressed by her beauty and, unlike
the rest of the drooling masses who have been throwing themselves at her all night, you do not have her on a pedestal. You show
her that you consider her to be just like any other girl, and she
should have to prove to *you* that she's worthy of *your* attention.
This is a tricky tightrope to walk, but it can be incredibly effective
when done right.

Also, understand that Strength of Character is a huge part of why
so many good girls tend to fall for bad boys. Bad boys don't take, put
up with, or fall for any of their shit. Women often see this as a display
of Alpha Male strength, and it stokes their attraction engines. The
truth may be that he is a self-centered asshole who genuinely doesn't
care about her, but that is overridden by the fact that he won't bow
down and let her control him. (You may think women want control
in a relationship—a belief that's perpetuated by the Dopey, Weak
Male/Beautiful, Strong Female couples on sitcoms, something I call
the "Jim Belushi Effect"—but they don't. They want a man who is in
control, and who doesn't let them walk all over him. Sorry, Jim.) So
when she's shitty to you, stick to your guns. And don't reward her
behavior by becoming her "yes" man. It only lowers your value.

LOYALTY

Back in Chapter 1, we went over the rules of being a good wing-man, one of which was: Always have your buddy's back. This is not only a rule to live by if you're out to score chicks, it's also essential if you want to build attraction. Women are masters at reconnaissance. They are constantly observing and gathering intel—and part of the intel she wants to gather on you is how faithful and loyal you are to your friends. How do you treat them? How do you behave with them? What do you say about them when they're not around? Would you be there for them if push came to shove? A man who has strong ties of loyalty to his friends, family, cowork-ers, and teammates is extremely sexy to a woman because she knows that a guy who is loyal to those around him will most likely be loyal to her too. She also knows all too well that weasels who lie, cheat, and backstab their friends wouldn't hesitate to do the same to her—so she'll be looking to how you treat your friends for clues as to how you would be as a mate.

Nice Guys, if you really want to show her that you're a good guy, do it by being loyal to the people around you *who have earned it*. That's important. Loyalty is something that's earned. You're loyal to your buddies because they've covered your ass more times than ESPN has covered Brett Favre's retirement. And you, in turn, have covered theirs. You've earned each other's loy-alty, but she hasn't earned yours yet. So, while it's perfectly okay to fight the crowd at the bar to grab your boys another round or to change your opinion or view on a topic to jump to your buddy's defense in an argument, it's not okay to do that for the sake of try-ing to bed some chick you've just met.

And, trust me, a woman will try to get you to turn on your brothers and see if you'll say anything bad about them, or give up any embarrassing info. She wants to see if your desire to get her to like you trumps your loyalty to your friends. It's just another of her Shit Tests. And if you do turn on your boys thinking it'll sway her to like you, not only will she see you for the traitor you are, but your boys won't be too happy with you either. "Bros before hos" doesn't seem like a lame frat-boy rallying cry anymore, does it? So keep the motto of the U.S. Marines in mind: *Semper Fidelis.* Always Faithful. You must be loyal to those who have earned it above all else. And make sure she knows that she has to earn it too.

As a side note, Sun Tzu had a very effective way of building loyalty among his men. To keep them willing to do whatever was necessary in battle, he said, "When you capture spoils from the enemy, they must be used as rewards, so that all your men may have a desire to fight." Do the same for your wingmen. If you're in a set and doing well, pull them in and introduce them to the women with whom you're engaging. Spread the female spoils around. The guys who aren't as good at meeting women will appreciate it and be motivated to return the favor. The women will notice what you've done as well, which only raises your value in their eyes— and keeps that attraction engine humming.

FEARLESSNESS

I could also have called this characteristic "Balls," or "Brass," or even "Cojones." Any one of them would have been appropriate. Ask yourself this question: Are you a risk taker? Not a crazy hey-y'all-watch-this-and-jump-off-a-roof-into-a-puddle-of-water risk taker, but a guy who takes calculated risks and does things most guys wouldn't dare do. Why do I ask? Because women love risk takers.

Think about the guys women always say they love: soldiers/cops/firemen. You know, the typical "hot guy" careers that all have their own Sexy Shirtless Whatever calendars every year. I'm sure there are plenty of great looking air conditioning repairmen out there too, but chicks aren't scrambling to buy a Hot Dudes with Freon calendar. Of course, women will say it's because they love a man in uniform, but the truth is that it's more about what the uniform stands for. Most people run from danger; these guys choose to run *toward* it. And that daily show of courage in the face of death makes women go weak in the knees. (And has an effect on certain other areas of their bodies as well.) It's also the second part of the reason why chicks love bad boys. Your typical bad boy isn't afraid of anything and takes a lot of risks.

Think about the bad boy vehicle of choice: the motorcycle. They are one of the riskiest vehicles you can drive, and women happen to find them incredibly sexy. It's the same with tattoos. A lot of women find ink irresistible. Is it because the sight of a well-executed tribal dragon makes their loins twitch? No. Again, it's because the typical personality traits of the guys who get tattoos—rebellious, impulsive, strong-minded, bold, risk taking—fall right in line with what fuels her attraction.

Does this mean I want you to run out and buy a Harley, or go have "Mom" tattooed on your arm? Not at all. You can show a woman you've got balls not just by taking physical risks, but by taking *social* risks. For instance, it can be as simple as following a girl onto a crowded dance floor—sober, and in front of your buddies—or even just approaching a hot woman when she's surrounded by a group of friends. That is a huge social risk. One many guys don't have the cojones to try.

You can also take social risks by the way you dress, also known as "peacocking." Like a peacock attracts a mate by a show of ostentatious plumage, veteran pick up artists would go out into the field in ridiculous, attention grabbing outfits: crazy hats, brightly colored shirts, lots of jewelry, or even feather boas. They reported back that chicks were drawn to them because they stood out and commanded attention. Which is true. It's difficult to go unnoticed in a sports bar when wearing a top hat and feather boa, but it also takes balls of steel to walk into that crowded sports bar in a top hat and feather boa. Women, consciously or subconsciously, sense that social fearlessness.

While you can decide for yourself if peacocking is your thing or not, I recommend you make a conscious effort to stand out from the crowd when you head out. If you dress like everyone else, you'll just blend into everyone else. You need to give women a reason to notice you. So, whatever it is that helps you turn heads, do it. Bright pink shirt? Some guys can pull that off like a champ. Fedora? Chicks dig guys in hats—and they *always* come over and ask if they can try them on. You can use jewelry, piercings, unusually colored socks, attention-grabbing belt buckles, whatever you feel helps you stand out. Even an oversized watch can work. I have one I got at a flea market that looks like an expensive European designer watch and, no matter what bar I'm at, in whatever city I'm in, women come over and ask to see it. It's actually one of my best openers.

WAR STORY: CHUCK, A BED, AND THE TWIN HOTTIES

I heard this story at that Miami dating class I attended: A recently divorced guy in his early fifties who I'll call "Chuck," had just spent the better part of the night on a poolside bed with not one, but two, incredibly hot chicks about twenty-five years his junior. All the guys in the class agreed they were by far the hottest targets any of them had seen that weekend.

Chuck had just been shot down for the second or third time and went over to one of the instructors to tell him he was done for the night. He wasn't getting it and he didn't feel like suffering any more rejection and embarrassment. The instructor's response was to drag him over to where these two women were and physically push him into the set.

Not only was Chuck much older than most everyone at the bar, he was also nearly completely bald, not exactly physically fit, and had a pasty skin tone. In addition, his sense of style could only be described as "discount-store sensible," which only made him more self-conscious among the fashion-conscious South Beach glamour crowd in attendance. Plus, he hadn't been on a date in over twenty years, and had just been shot down by two or three far less attractive girls. You could say he was just a little nervous.

So there he was, thrust onto the bed, right in between the Twin Hotties who were in mid conversation. I'm not sure who was more shocked: them or him. But he asked one of his Opinion Openers (which I'll explain in Chapter 4), and just started talking to them. Eventually he relaxed as he realized they were not only interested in what he had to say, but were easy to talk to despite their supermodel looks. No longer intimidated, he ended up talking to them until the pool bar closed several hours later.

They all got up to say goodnight, when one of them took his hand and asked him if he wanted to come upstairs to her room "to continue the conversation." The hottest chick by far this guy had ever seen—much less spoken to—had just invited him back to her hotel room while dozens of male models were roaming the hotel grounds alone.

I wish I could report that he went with her and had the kind of night that makes the Penthouse Forum editor weep with joy, but not so. He declined. He hadn't been with a woman "in that way" other than his ex-wife in over twenty years and was concerned about having "performance anxiety" and embarrassing himself. Which I completely understand and give him props for admitting. As far as I'm concerned, just having the hottest woman in the room invite you back to her room is victory enough.

So how did a balding, doughy, average-looking older guy who wasn't in possession of a Trump-sized bank account get the hottest woman on South Beach to offer to swing open the door to her hotel room—among other things? Simple. He showed Fearlessness by being the only guy that entire night to have the balls to approach her.

Now, had he just stopped there, he would have been like every other d-bag who normally approaches this type of hot woman by plopping down, forcing his way into the conversation, and have nothing to say or offer. But Chuck actually had interesting things to say and directed the conversation. He had a ton of mental strength, and the ladies appreciated that. Add in the fact that he showed his strength of character by not overtly hitting on them, agreeing to everything they said, or playing "yes" man, and that he relaxed and didn't constantly tell them how beautiful they were or that he couldn't believe he was actually talking to them (which instantly lowers your value. More on that in Chapter 7.), and you have the makings of a very successful mission. And trust me, if Chuck can pull chicks like that by hitting all their attraction buttons, you can too.

THE LAW OF ATTRACTION

If wielded properly, attraction will be your most powerful weapon. So powerful that, unlike opening lines and other typical pickup techniques, she won't even know you're using it. Or realize she's falling for it—and for you. Your sword stays sheathed, her defense mechanisms stay in the "off" position, and the battle can be won without a single shot being fired—which means less chance of being shot down.

Sun Tzu says, "If you know the enemy and know yourself, you need not fear the results of a hundred battles. If you know yourself, but not the enemy, for every victory gained you will also suffer a defeat. If you know neither the enemy nor yourself, you will succumb in every battle." Before you cracked open this book, you may have known nothing about women, what attracts them, and what strategies to use to get past their defenses, much less known what type of guy you had to be in order to see results. Since you knew neither the enemy nor yourself, you may not have been very successful.

By this point you should know yourself and a little more about the enemy, but you still don't know enough to be victorious every time. Just being "attractive" isn't enough; you're going to have to employ some other strategies and tactics if you want to really get to know the women you're dealing with. So you need not fear the result of those hundred battles.

- If you want to win the battle without unsheathing your sword, (and without her raising her Bitch Shield), it's important to exhibit The Top Three Male Characteristics that Fuel Her Attraction Engine:
- Strength: This has nothing to do with physical strength. It's three very specific types of strength:

  1. Mental Strength: This is the ability to be Engaging, Exciting, Interesting, and Entertaining.
  2. Social Strength: Incredibly powerful. Just like a kid with a toy, if a woman sees other women enjoying "playing" with you, she's gonna want to play too.
  3. Strength of Character: Got swagger? Women love a guy who has self-confidence and backbone. Not a guy who bows to their will. Or their Shit Tests. This is where "Nice Guys" fail the most. And it's also part of why good girls fall for bad boys.

- Loyalty: She wants to know how faithful you are to your buddy. And if you have his back. Because she wants to know, if push came to shove, would you be there for her. But loyalty must be earned. Your buddies earned it, and she'll have to earn it too. And after she's earned it, then you can be a Nice Guy.
- Fearlessness: Women love risk takers, and those who have the courage and ability to protect them. You don't have to jump out of a plane to show her you're fearless. You can do it by taking social risks.

CHAPTER 4

TACTICS

"It is the same in love as in war."

—Marguerite De Valois

Sun Tzu wrote, "The good fighters of old first put themselves beyond the possibility of defeat, and then waited for an opportunity of defeating the enemy. Security against defeat implies defensive tactics; ability to defeat the enemy means taking the offensive. Standing on the defensive indicates insufficient strength; attacking, a superabundance of strength."

Sun Tzu wasn't one to sit back, wait, and give his opponent a shot at the upper hand. He believed the key to victory lay in taking the offensive—and you should too. Why? Because making the first move puts you in control of the situation. You decide when and where the first shots get fired. You decide the direction the first interaction takes. And you decide how to put yourself beyond the possibility of defeat. These are all valuable strategic advantages that you'll need when women start using their Shit Tests and Bitch Shields, and every other weapon at their disposal, to try and throw you off your game.

When you, or the guys you know, hang out in bars, how many of you have the spine to just walk over to a hot babe and initiate a conversation? I'm going to go ahead and guess the answer is "not a whole lot." Most guys will hang back, check over and over again to see if a girl looks interested, and ponder whether to approach, or wait until she makes her way over to talk to them. You may think this is a great situation—she must like you, she came over to talk to you, so you're in—but it actually puts you in the defensive position. You have a much better chance of succeeding if you take the offensive and control your entire approach.

LEARN THE WHEN AND HOW

Your approach is the When and How of your first engagement with your target, and it's where a lot of guys tend to get shot down before they even set foot on the battlefield. Every time I watch guys approach women in bars—knowing that they are just going to get blown out of the water—it reminds me of that opening scene from *Saving Private Ryan* where mobs of soldiers pour out of the Higgins boats into the water while storming Omaha Beach. Those guys were picked off left and right before they even got their feet wet—let alone got a shot off—and it's the same with your approach. It doesn't matter if you're the greatest, most entertaining guy ever to slide on a pair of jeans. If you blow the approach and just go running at her with no plan and your rifle half cocked, she'll take you out before you even open your mouth.

THE WHEN

I mentioned that your approach includes the "When." Almost every dating coach, pickup artist, cocksman, swordsman, and armchair Romeo will tell you that you must abide by the Three Second Rule: If you spot a hot babe, you have to approach her within three seconds. No staring soulfully across the bar, trying to catch her eye. No walking to the bathroom every fifteen minutes, just to pass by her and see if she smiles. You see her, you approach—immediately.

Why? Two reasons. One, this rule doesn't give you the chance to wuss out and think of a million reasons why you shouldn't talk to her. Two, it shows confidence; you're a man who goes after what he wants. You saw her, and you just had to go over and talk to her. You show no fear—and that's like hitting the throttle on her attraction engine. So if you see her and you like her, approach right then and there, before your balls shrink to the size of peas, and you decide that, instead of the dream girl you've been hoping for, she's a psycho bitch who will ruin your life and run off with your best friend, your dog, and your *Mad Men* Complete Season One DVDs.

THE HOW

The How of your approach is also important. You want to be very confident and deliberate because, from the second she sees you coming toward her, she's already started to form an opinion of you in her head. And what's helping her do that is your body language. If you walk over and appear in any way to be timid, nervous, or insecure, you might as well be a wounded gazelle limping into a lion's den—only the gazelle probably has a better shot at survival. Women can smell fear—almost as quickly as they can spot cheap shoes and a fake Rolex.

Believe me, I understand that, at the beginning, walking up to a seriously hot woman can be more terrifying than waking up naked, tied to Courtney Love's bed, but that doesn't mean you have to let her know that. Think of it this way: Have you ever been in a large city where there are a lot of pan handlers? After hearing the same pitch for spare change over and over, you start to recognize the body language of a panhandler and become aware of them approaching from the corner of your eye. So the second you hear, "Excuse me, sir, but could you . . ." you already know what's coming because you've heard it all before. It's not that you don't have compassion for them; you're just tired of the intrusion and the same old sad story. It's the same with women.

In this scenario, men are the panhandlers, only we're begging for phone numbers and sex instead of change. Women have seen the same approach, and heard the same lines, over and over again. They are tired of the intrusion, so you need to approach with different body language, and have a sharper and more interesting opener than any other guy who has tried before you.

BODY LANGUAGE

You've heard the old saying "actions speak louder than words," right? Well, your body language speaks even louder than your actions. How you walk, how you stand in a bar, even how you hold your beer, can say more about you to the women you're trying to meet than anything that comes out of your mouth—no matter how clever and polished it may be.

A few basic body language tips: Check your posture and make sure you're standing tall. Hunching over is a telltale sign of insecurity, plus it makes you look sad or depressed. Would you want some sad or depressed dude coming over to talk to you when you're out having a good time? Of course not. You'd do whatever you could to avoid him or get rid of him as soon as possible. So would she.

You also want to be conscious of your facial expressions. When you go up to her, you don't want to look scared or anxious, like you're about to hear the results of her pregnancy test. Instead, show her that you're fun, confident, and exciting by smiling. And try for a relaxed smile that says you're about to turn her night into the most fun and memorable one she's had in a while, not a forced, creepy, smile that only offers up the possibility she may wake up in your basement chained to a gurney with a bird cage on her head.

You want to be cool, calm, and collected when you approach a woman. Avoid appearing overly eager or exuberant because it makes it look like you've never been in the presence of a hot woman before—or like you just got done doing a long stretch in the state pen. Understandably, chicks find that a little unnerving. Also, guys who make quick, sharp movements around women run a risk of making them very nervous. Yes, you want to be excited to meet her, but dial it down a little. If you're a Type A personality, or have the disposition of a Jack Russell Terrier, and have a tough time doing that, use this trick: Imagine you're underwater. It'll help you slow everything down and make your movements more deliberate—and more appealing.

THE DRINK SHIELD

It's obvious now that body language has a huge effect on social interaction—especially when it comes to getting laid—but most guys don't know that even something as subtle and unconscious as how we hold our beers can trip a defensive signal to women.

The next time you're in a bar, take a look around at the guys who are standing around drinking, and notice where they are holding their beers. If you look closely, you'll see that the confident ones who show a little swagger and have an easy time talking to women tend to be relaxed and hold their drinks casually down by their sides. But guys who are uncomfortable or insecure hold their beers in front of their chests, like protective Drink Shields, warding off incoming social situations. Women subconsciously pick up on this and can read it as fear, or they think you're being standoffish, don't really want to interact with them, or any number of other negative messages.

Think of it this way: If you were going to talk to a chick (or anyone else for that matter) for the first time, would you stand there with your arms crossed in front of you? Of course not. You wouldn't do that when talking to your boss or a client. It's rude, and looks like you're trying to block them out by putting a wall up between the two of you. It's probably the least inviting body position you can take. Well, a Drink Shield is similar body language, just not as pronounced. So the next time you're standing in a bar holding a drink, keep it at your side. You don't want a Drink Shield to block out the ladies.

RESPECT HER PERSONAL SPACE

When you approach a woman, don't invade her personal space or even make her think you're going to; this can put her immediately on the defensive. When guys go up to other guys, we usually walk straight up, shoulders squared. It's part of our ingrained body language. We try to "out Alpha" the other guy, show our strength, and show that we're not intimidated. You don't want a woman to feel threatened as you approach, so pay attention to what you're doing. A lot of guys walk up to women straight on, which can make them feel uncomfortable and intimidated— especially if the guy is much bigger than she is and approaches her aggressively. In her mind, he's not trying to get to know her or show her a good time, instead he's trying to dominate her. Which everyone knows isn't supposed to happen until the third date when she puts on the leather mask and ball gag, and he pulls out the whips.

So what can you do? Easy: Approach from an angle and turn your body slightly so you're not in such an aggressive "squared shoulder" position. An interesting technique that I've tried and like a lot is something I like to call the "You Stopped Me on My Way to Somewhere Else" maneuver. This is where you act like you were going to walk past her, but something about her stopped you in your tracks and you had to take a minute to talk to her. You didn't make a bee line for her; your body is past hers and still aimed in the direction you were going, and you're talking to her over your shoulder. You're not invading her personal space and she didn't think you were coming in to hit on her, so she didn't get the chance to form an opinion of you or get her defenses ready. It seems like a casual encounter, and since you're on your way somewhere else, she doesn't feel like you're planning on hanging around the whole night. (This is a perfect "False Time Constraint," something I explain in Chapter 5.) Then you can slowly turn and face her when she's comfortable and turns to face you.

So remember, when those three seconds are ticking, and you're heading toward that hot chick, you must have the mindset that you are the greatest guy she is ever going to meet. You're going to make her night fun and exciting. You are confident and self-assured. So, make sure your face doesn't show the terror you may be feeling and don't come at her like you're about to hip check her into the boards.

WAR STORY: IF YOU STARE LONG ENOUGH, THEY WILL COME. SORT OF . . .

Years ago, way before I understood anything at all about the Art of War for Dating, I made just about every mistake you could possibly make when it came to meeting women. This particular story happened during my lean years when the closest thing I had to a date was when my mom took me shopping for college dorm supplies and we'd stop for lunch on the way home.

Over summer break, everyone would hang out on this one particular street that was home to eight or nine bars and clubs, each more of a dive and more packed than the next. Since my buddies and I weren't exactly Casanovas, we'd spend the summer months drinking beer and checking out girls. There was one girl I checked out more than any other. Her name was Amber and she was the most beautiful girl I had ever seen. No exaggeration. She was one of those goddesses who only comes along once in a lifetime. Like a walking, talking centerfold with perfect blond hair, and the biggest, bluest eyes you have ever seen. She turned every head in that bar every single night. And she drove me insane.

She was dating the resident DJ, who was from a wealthy, powerful family; I was completely intimidated, and everything about my body language showed it. I figured I had no shot, and resigned myself to admiring her from afar, which I did for two whole summers. Sad, I know.

One day my buddy Eddie and I made our way through the bar and, as usual, found a spot where I could get a clear visual shot at Amber. Only this night we noticed that Amber and her hot friend Dawn, were looking back at us—and smiling. Eddie and I looked at each other. Holy shit! Were Amber and Dawn smiling at us? We looked back over. Now they were looking at us and giggling and whispering to each other. I looked behind me, thinking they had to be looking at some other guy. Maybe DJ Rich and Powerful was back there. Nope; when I turned back around Dawn was making her way toward us, and Amber was looking dead at me. Had my two years of lamely trying to make eye contact finally worked? Had I worn her down enough to where she just had to know who I was?

"Hi," said Dawn, now standing in front of me.

"Um, hi." (I was a master conversationalist.)

"We just wanted you to know that your friend right there
. . . ." (She was pointing at Eddie. "Shit. Did Amber like him
instead of me? He was a good-looking guy. Had she been digging
him all this time? My mind was racing and my mouth went dry.
Adrenaline was pumping through my body. I love Eddie, but if he
ends up with her instead of me, I swear . . ."

Then she finished her sentence:

". . . is standing in vomit."

We looked down. And sure enough, Eddie was standing in a
pile of freshly offered regurgitation. Apparently it happened right
before we got there. And Amber and Dawn had watched it happen, and then watched us blindly walk over and stand in it.

"Um, thanks."

That was all I could get out. After two years, I finally had the
chance to say something to them, to let them see what a fun,
interesting, witty guy I was, and all I could say was "Um, thanks."
Dawn just looked at me with that come-on-you-can-do-better-
than-that look on her face. But I had nothing. I was like a deer
caught in the headlights. She threw me a lifeline, and I let it sail
over my head. She rolled her eyes and walked away.

See, as much I had wanted to talk to Amber, I wanted her to
initiate the conversation because I was too much of a pussy to do
it myself. I was afraid she'd reject me, so I figured the only way
I would know for sure if she liked me was if *she* came over to
me. But like Sun Tzu said, "The ability to defeat the enemy
means taking the offensive. Standing on the defensive indicates
insufficient strength." When they put me on the defensive by
actually walking over, I was completely caught off guard. I wasn't
in control of the situation. Didn't have any kind of witty comeback.

Instead I just froze. The battle was quick and decisive, and I was the only casualty—besides Eddie's shoes.

It can't be stressed enough: You need to be the one who takes the offensive and initiates contact whenever possible. You need to make her feel comfortable and not intimidate her. And finally, you need to have the ability to portray who you are and what you're about, before you even open your mouth.

- Put yourself "beyond the possibility of defeat" by taking the offensive. Why? Because being on the defensive is a show of weakness. It shuts down your ability to make her want you, and keeps you from controlling the situation.
- Your approach is the When and How of your first engagement with her. When? Within three seconds of first seeing her, before you have a chance to talk yourself out of it. How? Confidently and deliberately. Without intimidating her or making her think you're going to hip check her into the boards.
- Body language is crucial to social interaction . . . especially when it comes to getting laid.
- Don't approach a woman like a panhandler, begging for attention and sex.
- Stop hiding behind the Drink Shield. Holding your beer in front of your chest is your body's way of screaming, "Stay away from me! I'm nervous!"

CHAPTER 5
ENERGY

"A woman begins by resisting a man's advances and ends up blocking his retreat."

—Oscar Wilde

Once you've approached a woman successfully, you'll need to "open" her; that is, use an "opener" to break the ice and get her talking. Notice I said opener and not "pickup line." Pick up lines are what lounge prowlers use to try to get barflies to join them in the men's room stall. An opener is something that sparks an actual conversation that you'll use to not only get to know a woman, but to get a reaction, like making her laugh or think or give an opinion so you can begin building attraction. And, since you're taking the offensive here, you get to strategize how the encounter goes. But unless your summer blockbuster action movie just opened that weekend, or you're approaching her from the deck of your mega-yacht, you're going to need to open her with something more than, "'Sup?"

Sun Tzu demanded that his generals be decisive and not waver in the heat of battle. That's what gets good men sent home with arrows in their asses. He says, "The Good fighter will be terrible in his onset, and prompt in his decision. Energy may be likened to the bending of a crossbow; decision to the releasing of the trigger." You can't release an arrow halfway. You can't sort of shoot a crossbow. When you decide to pull the trigger, it shoots forward at full force; there's no middle ground.

It's the same with your opener. Think of your approach as the bending of the crossbow and your opener as the pulling of the trigger; you can't do it halfway. Once you've crossed that crowded bar and are standing in front of her, you have to "be terrible in your onset" and hit her with the best you've got. This is not the time to half-ass it. Many men have gone up to a woman and "sort of" talked to her or "kind of" started a conversation; all of these men have been sent home with hot babe–launched arrows in their asses.

REHEARSE YOUR LINES

Considering a lot of guys get nervous just walking over to a chick, the added pressure of actually talking to her can be seriously difficult. Nerves take over and, rather than a start to a conversation, the open becomes little more than a battle to stop stuttering and remember what the hell you were going to say. Sure you can do The Hit & Run 50 (See Chapter 2) to alleviate most of your approach anxiety, but it's perfectly normal to feel that adrenalin surge and rush of nerves when you go to open your mouth and deliver your opener; even veteran actors and musicians still get stage fright when they have to perform. But rather than let your nerves take over and blow your shot, memorize a couple of good openers that you're comfortable with. Then, when you do open her, it will come out naturally—no stuttering, stammering, or loading the sentences with "um" and "er" as if you're just getting a grasp on the English language. They should be so rehearsed as to not seem rehearsed at all.

Sun Tzu taught, "He wins his battles by making no mistakes. Making no mistakes is what establishes the certainty of victory, for it means conquering an enemy that is already defeated. Hence the skillful fighter puts himself in a position that makes defeat impossible . . . ." And how do you keep from making mistakes? By practicing—over and over again—until what you're saying is second nature because practice makes perfect.

USE PROVEN OPENERS

Even more important than practicing your openers is establishing the certainty of victory by using openers that have been proven to work, in the field, by guys who have tried them time and again— tweaking them, honing them, and polishing them—until they return successful results every time. (I give you a few to use in this chapter.) After all, why go in cold, wondering if she'll reject your opener, when there are hundreds of tried-and-true openers that'll work for you just as they worked for everyone who has used them before you? Might as well stack the odds in your favor.

Notice I said "reject your opener" and not "reject you"? She doesn't even know you yet, so how could she be rejecting you personally? Remember, women have been fighting off advances since they were old enough to vote, if not earlier. And the hotter they are (and obviously you want your targets to fall into the "hot" category), the more often they'll hear some sort of pick up line from a guy. So blowing them off, ignoring them, or shooting them down has become second nature, a reflex. And if your opener doesn't cut through that clutter, she's going to instinctively reject it. Not you. Your opener. Keep that in mind and don't take the rejection of your opener as an attack on your looks, personality, or worth as a man—and you'll be more relaxed when you deliver your openers in the first place.

TYPES OF OPENERS

Sun Tzu said, "In battle, there are not more than two methods of attack—the direct and the indirect; yet these two in combination give rise to an endless series of maneuvers." And it is the same in opening; you can choose the direct or indirect open, and there are an infinite number of ways to do it.

The direct opener is where you walk up to a chick and say something like "Hi, I'm John. I saw you walk in, thought you were really cute, and I just wanted to come over and introduce myself." These types of openers are straight and to the point. You're not hiding your intentions at all. For obvious reasons, direct openers are much higher risk, and are used most often by guys who have self-confidence to spare, which, as you recall, is huge attraction fuel. So while the risk can be great, so can the rewards.

However, since there's not much to direct openers beyond having balls of steel and knowing how to use them, we are going to focus on indirect openers. Those are the ones you'll use to evade her defenses and get her into a conversation, without letting on that you are trying to pick her up. Sneaky? Maybe. Effective? More than you know.

See, your entire goal on these missions is to build attraction and get her comfortable with you. You can't do that if she shoots you down from the get go. For her to be attracted to you, you need to have a conversation. (And also to "qualify" her, and see if she's the kind of girl you'd want to date. We'll talk about that in detail in Chapter 6.) Indirect openers take away the worry of immediate rejection by not coming across as a pick up attempt, sneaking under her radar, and getting her talking to you. One of the most effective ways to do that is the opinion opener.

OPINION OPENERS

Have you ever met a woman without an opinion? An opinion she desperately wanted to share with you, whether you wanted her to or not? Of course not. Opinion-free women are like unicorns, jackalopes, and straight male flight attendants: they do not exist. Asking a woman to give you her opinion on something—anything— is like blowing a hole in the Hoover Dam. All you can do is just hang on and try to ride out the onslaught. This is especially true if you open a set of two or more women who have differing opinions.

See, if you come in and ask a question like "Can I buy you a drink?" or "Would you like to dance?" you give her the chance to say no, which is like rolling over and showing your belly. You put her in control, and give her the decision-making power along with the power to reject your approach. Instead, come in indirectly and say something like, "My friend and I were having an argument and we need a woman to help settle it: Is making out considered cheating?" or "Do drunk 'I love you's' count?" Instead of hitting on her and engaging her defenses, now all you're asking is for her assistance in solving a problem. And no woman can resist solving someone else's problem. It's like chick crack. And even if she's in Bitch-Shield mode and just answers a snippy "No" to a question like "Do drunk 'I love you's' count?" the "No" isn't directed at you—just at your question. You still have the opportunity to:

- Decide she's not for you and eject.
- Ask a follow-up question like "Well, why not? Is it because you can plead temporary insanity?"
- Start a debate to get her into conversation by telling her that you *do* think they count and here's why.

No matter which option you choose, you take control of the situation and conversation by putting yourself "beyond the possibility of defeat."

A quick note: If you want extra ammo to bring down her defensive shields, use a False Time Constraint. Saying something like, "I have to get right back to my friends, but I wanted your opinion on something . . ." or "My friends will be here in a minute but I wonder if you can answer a question for me . . ." lets her know that you plan on needing her attention for just a short time; you don't plan on hanging around all night. She'll be much more receptive when she's not thinking that you'll stick around asking questions for hours and intrude on her good time with her friends.

BE COCKY AND FUNNY

We know women are attracted to strong, confident men, so being just a little cocky when you approach, while taking the arrogant edge off with some humor, can be a very effective indirect opener. Not only do you cut through the usual crap she hears about how hot she is, but you position yourself as a guy who has a higher social value than she does. You're not begging for her approval. Instead, you're flipping it around and assuming that she already likes you; you're asking her to prove that *she's* worthy of talking to *you*. Sound risky? You'd be surprised at how safe it is—especially when the woman is seriously hot. Just because she's gorgeous doesn't mean she doesn't want to laugh and be entertained. (And if she doesn't, well, then you don't want to date her anyway.) A beautiful woman has probably heard some version of "Wow, do you know how hot you are?" at least two dozen times today, so a comment about how you want her to stop staring at your ass because it makes you feel like a piece of meat might catch her off guard and get her to laugh.

Naturally, this type of opener won't work if you have the personality of your average Department of Motor Vehicles worker. And, sure, you'll need much bigger balls to pull it off than you do with an opinion opener, but remember some of the things women find attractive: mental strength, strength of character, and fearlessness. Being cocky and funny hits all those points.

You show her that you're comfortable with yourself, have the confidence to stand toe-to-toe with her regardless of her looks, and aren't intimidated or overly impressed by attractive women. And depending on what you use to open, you can also challenge her mentally. Engage her in a little witty repartee. This is a helluva lot sexier to her than "God, you're so hot. Can I buy you a drink?"

CLASSIFIED INFO: FIELD-TESTED OPENERS

The good news is that, because they are so effective, great openers are widely shared, discussed, dissected, and traded. Guys all over the world use the most successful openers to get women talking and build attraction. This means that you can put tried and true openers into play immediately. No testing period necessary.

Now the bad news: Because of the recent fascination with, and resulting prevalence of, "Pickup Artists" in the mainstream media—in books, movies, online, and on TV—women have been able to do a ton of recon and know all the tricks. (I told you they were worthy adversaries.) They're wise to all different types of openers, and many women can recognize an opinion opener as a means to a pick up, rather than simply an innocent question, the second it's asked. Or, worse, they have been hit with the same opener several times in a night especially if it's one of the widely used ones you'll find here. If she calls you on it and you're not quick enough on your feet, this can turn your offensive advantage into a disadvantage in a heartbeat, putting you on the defensive as you scramble to explain yourself.

So I want you to use these following openers in two ways:

1. Use these truly successful gems to get your feet wet, get comfortable, and get positive results immediately.

2. Use them as building blocks to develop your own unique openers that won't have you running the risk of being the third guy that night to ask her if a drunk "I love you" counts.

My friend Bobby Rio compiled the following winning openers. Bobby is a dating coach who specializes in teaching guys how to turn ordinary conversations into sexy conversations and amp up the sexual tension. (Something we'll talk more about later in Chapter 8.) He has been collecting openers for years, and put 175 of the most effective ones into an e-book titled, *The Little Black Book of Openers*. (You can grab a free copy at *www.GreatSeducer .com*)

I've chosen a wide variety of openers in order to represent a mixture of "personalities;" it's important to choose the ones that fit your personality and work for you. Remember that the idea is to not just spit out some canned lines, but to be authentic and real. Be yourself, because the ultimate goal is to turn this into a real dating opportunity. You'll still have to transition into actual conversation after you open successfully, so if you come in with an opener that sets you up as this cocky, confident funnyman, but that's not you at all, she'll see through you and you won't stand a chance. (This is also why Chapter 6 is dedicated to transitioning.) So when you're deciding on which openers to practice and perfect, keep in mind that this is just the opening salvo in what will be a longer overall battle.

Note: The following openers are used with permission from The Little Black Book of Openers by Bobby Rio. Credit is given to the originator whenever possible. Edits made for spelling, grammar, and clarity when necessary.

OPINION OPENERS

JEN OR ANGELINA?

You: "Hey I need your opinion about something. If you were Brad Pitt, who would you choose? Angelina or Jennifer?"

Them: (Whoever . . . although it's usually Angelina.)

You: "How funny, my friend said 'Jennifer.' He said because she's 'safe' but who picks safe over sexy right?"

This works great if there are two or more girls in the set. When one of them becomes an obstacle, you can tease her about being the "safe" one.

You: "Oh I get it! You're the 'safe' one! I'm going to call you Jennifer from now on (laugh). Hey Jennifer, I'm going to hang out with Angelina for a bit, she's the fun one."

ORAL SEX (ORIGINATED BY BADBOY)

You: "Hey girls, Let me ask you something. (Pause.) Oral sex on first date (pause). Yes or No?"

They'll get shocked because you are so bold. You should follow up with a story:

"See, they did a study about this in Cambridge, and they found out that couples that had oral sex on the first date stayed together a very, very long time. Some of them even got married. I have this date tomorrow, and I would like to have some with her, but I really don't want to get married. Do you believe in this bullshit, or do you follow your instincts?"

Changing topic from here is very easy.

DENTAL FLOSS (ORIGINATED BY STYLE AND MYSTERY)

You: "Hey guys, I need to get your opinion on something. It's very important, and we need a woman's perspective. It's a matter of life and death. My friend and I were having a debate and your answer could completely change my entire life. Do you brush before flossing or floss before brushing? No one knows . . ."

MOTORCYCLE (ORIGINATED BY LUCKY13)

You: "I need a female opinion. My buddy (put hand on wing-man's shoulder) wants to get a bike (motorcycle). Could he get more chicks with a crotch rocket or a Harley?"

Each girl has her opinion and at least one will answer directly to the wingman, while the others start asking what you ride. They'll all want rides and you can always get a number close, a type of close meaning you got her number as opposed to a kiss in a kiss close, or sex in a sex close, etc. (See the Glossary at the end of the book for a more complete definition.) I know what you're thinking. "But I don't have a bike." It's not a problem. When she asks, "What do you ride?" (And she will) just pull back with a humble:

"Oh I'm just learning. I can't take you out yet." *Then switch to,* "So girls jump on the back of strangers' bikes all the time, but getting in a less lethal *car* with a stranger is 'dangerous.' What's up with that?" *And go from there.*

BLONDE HAIR (ORIGINATED BY TYLER DURDEN)

You: "Ladies, get this. I need an opinion."

Them: "What?"

You: "I'm thinking of dying my hair *totally blonde.*"

Them: "No. Yes. No." (They debate.)

You: "How about like this . . . streaks . . . etc."

This transitions easily into "I'm going on TV. The Jerry Springer show." or many other routines. Just pre-plan it, and it can go anywhere.

MIME (ORIGINATED BY AUTHORITARIANIST)

You: "I need an opinion on something." (Touch her on the elbow to get her attention.)

Her: (Leans in closer.)

You: "I'm thinking about quitting my job and becoming a mime."

Her: (Smile or cracks up.)

You: "When you see me doing my thing, will you put a dollar (say "euro" if you want to appear well-traveled) in my hat?"

Her: "I don't know are you any good?"

You: "I'm the best. I have an edge on all the other mimes out there. (Pause and make eye contact.) I talk!"

Then go into how you're going to spirit her away to some exotic foreign capital where you will mime while she picks the pockets of gawking tourists. Add that after stowing the loot you'll both streak through fancy museums all jacked up on Red Bull and ecstasy. By this time she should be laughing her ass off.

COCKY FUNNY
TRAINING OPENERS (ORIGINATED BY RICHARD LA RUINA)
Use these different openers to open a set.

"I know you probably get no attention from guys whatsoever, so I thought I'd come and make some conversation with you."

- *"Which of you guys gets hit on the most?"* (For a set of two hot babes.)
- *"Are you confident enough to accept a sincere compliment? Good, so am I, you go first."*

RICH OPENER (ORIGINATED BY HERBAL, TD)

When opening a set, walk up and ask, "Which one of you is the richest?" *Then go into the whole* "Okay, you get to be my sugar mama, then. But, hmm . . . we need someone to cook for us, who is the best cook?" *routine. Take it from there.*

CELL PHONE OPENER

Say you're on a bus/train/airport shuttle, sitting next to a hot babe and there's no good excuse to start talking. Take out your cell phone, pretend to call someone, and have a fictitious (short) conversation. Look her in the eyes and say to your fictitious friend:

"Yeah, it's always the same story, girls keep ogling me. Yeah, there's one in front of me doing that right now. And you know what the worst part is? She's shy. Yeah, she's shy. She's been looking at me for like ten minutes and she hasn't even started a conversation yet! Okay, I mean, at least I appreciate the fact that she has a *lot* of self control; she hasn't tried to feel me up so far." *If she's not laughing by this point, she's no fun anyway.*

HOTTEST GIRL

Walk up to a girl/set and say:

"I lost a bet and I have to come here and ask the hottest girl on a date. Who do you girls think is the hottest girl in this damn place?"

THE TEST

You: "Congratulations."

Her: "Huh?"

You: "You passed my first test: You look (*or you dress*) interesting, which made me come here and talk to you. Now I want to know if you're fun."

NICE ASS OPENER

You: "Hey a girl just commented that I had a nice ass. It's hard for me to tell myself. (*Have her look at your ass and give an opinion.*) Give me a look at your ass. (*Make her turn around, give her the once over, and make a comment.*) Something like, I think mine is nicer. So, what do you think makes a good ass?"

FUN GENERAL OPENERS

BANK ROBBERY (ORIGINATED BY BADBOY)

Delivery must be playful.

You: "Hey girls, let me ask you something: Can you keep a secret?"

Them: "Yes."

You: "Okay, are you good drivers? Me and (friend's name) are robbing the bank across the street, and guess what? (Pause.) The driver screwed us. All you need to do is pick us up at 2:00 AM, and drive us to the airport. You get 3 percent."

This always leads into good conversation, with good energy. They always want to negotiate their percentage. They'll ask for 5 percent, 7 percent, etc. Just keep it going from there.

MIXED SET OPENERS (ORIGINATED BY JUGGLER)

A mixed set is a set that has male as well as female members. These openers are great to get you into the group and talking to your target, without her friends going into "protection mode."

"It's interesting that when you have a group of four or more people together like this, the tallest always stands across from the shortest." (*Or blondes across from brunettes, or boy-girl-boy-girl, etc. Alter as needed.*)

- "Who is the leader here? *(They all point.) Say playfully to leader,* What qualifies you to be in charge?" (*Add assorted humorous challenges to his/her leadership.*)
- "Do you guys want to see a magic trick? Alright, close your eyes." *(Take cute girl by the hand away from the group while everybody's eyes are closed. Do not return.)*
- "You see that group over there? They said they are more fun than your group. Please prove to me they are mistaken."
- "Where have I seen you guys before? Were you at (so and so's) party? The one where the stripper gave a lap dance to the clown?"
- *Count the number of people in the group (for example, let's say it's eight) Say to them:* "Don't you guys know that eight is an unlucky number?" *Then add:* "Good thing I'm here otherwise you would all be cursed to damnation."

WAR STORY: You Don't Have to be at the Tables to Win in Vegas

A few years ago, I was in Las Vegas with the editor of a magazine I was working for. We flew in late, so we went to a casino bar to have dinner and unwind a bit. A day or so earlier, she had interviewed Neil Strauss about his just-released book, *The Game,* probably the most in-depth look at the underground society of pick up artists ever written. During the interview, Strauss gave her some info on openers, and explained how certain ones, like Opinion Openers, can be very effective for dodging a woman's defenses and getting her into a conversation.

Over dinner, she told me she was skeptical, that it all sounded like bullshit and hype to sell books, but I was convinced his openers would work. A debate ensued. As we finished eating, I proposed an experiment. All during dinner, I noticed there were two hot babes sitting at the bar, trying to enjoy their drinks, while two guys desperately tried to pick them up. They bought drink after drink, told the women how beautiful they were, and laughed loudly at anything they said, but you could tell these chicks were hardcore Vegas vets. Jaded party girls just looking for some suckers to fund their night out. So it was shockingly obvious to everyone but the two chumps that these babes had no interest in them, except maybe as human cocktail dispensers.

So here was the challenge: I told my editor I could walk over to the girls and not only open them within seconds, but keep the conversation going long enough to get at least one phone number—maybe both. And, just to make the bet more interesting, I bet that I could get *them* to buy *us* a round of drinks. If I could succeed on both challenges, my editor would buy the dinner we just enjoyed. If I got shot down, the next three dinners were on me. The only rule? She had to go along with whatever I said. She would have to be my faithful wingwoman on this mission. No trying to sabotage me. Being that this was Vegas, and I was giving her three to one odds, she agreed and took the bet. Game on.

I walked over to the crowded bar, said to the chumps, "Excuse me, I just want to grab a drink for me and my friend," and sandwiched myself right between them and the hot babes. In all honesty, I was sweating like Tiger Woods in divorce court. This was the first time I had ever approached a set of women like this, let alone two this hot. And not only was I doing it with money on the line, I was pretty sure that, if I flamed out, my editor would add that to her piece on Strauss, proving his stuff doesn't work. There's nothing like the added pressure of public humiliation in print.

While waiting for the bartender to mix a vodka martini and a gin and tonic, I turned to the babes and hit them with one of the opinion openers I remembered from the book: "Hey you two look like you'd be pretty knowledgeable in this area. My friend here just got out of a very long-term relationship that ended badly. And because we happen to be in Vegas on business, a friend of hers fixed her up on a blind date with a professional gambler she knows. Now, she wants to go because it sounds 'exciting,' but I think it's a really bad idea. What do you think?"

Boom. I barely got that last sentence out, when the two of them launched into a verbal barrage unlike anything I've ever witnessed. They were firing questions, offering advice, and telling personal stories; they were like the hosts of *The View* on Red Bull. After only a few minutes of this, the chumps slinked their way over to the other side of the bar with their tails between their legs. (Sorry for the cockblock fellas, but I had a bet to win.) About twenty minutes in, I joked that they needed to buy the next round of drinks because we were the most interesting thing that happened to them that night, and had "rescued" them from the Chump Brothers. (Yeah, a real reach, but I couldn't think of anything else. Lame as it was, it worked anyway. Round of martinis and G&Ts on the hot babes.)

After forty minutes of them giving advice on everything from whether to accept blind dates, to how to dress for blind dates, to how to handle really bad blind dates, I said, "You guys were fantastic, and we really appreciate all your help, but we have to get up early tomorrow morning to get to our first appointment. But I'd really love to continue this conversation sometime." That's when they asked for something to write on so they could give us their phone numbers. They wanted us to call after the "date" so they could hear how it went.

Final score: One conversation with two hot babes. One round of drinks bought and paid for by a pair of veteran Vegas party girls. Two very desirable phone numbers. One free dinner from my editor. And one extra large portion of "I Told You So," served cold. I love Vegas.

Sun Tzu said, "The energy developed by good fighting men is as the momentum of a round stone rolled down a mountain thousands of feet in height." A good opener has the same energy; it crashes through her defenses with the momentum of that stone, giving you the opportunity to show her who you are. But it's what you do once you're in, that makes the difference between finishing the night with some late-night grease-fest at the diner with the guys, or finishing it with breakfast at her place. In the following chapter, you'll learn the next steps to making that happen.

- Once you've approached a woman, you need to "open" her to break the ice and get her talking. Openers spark conversation and allow you to take the offensive.

- Openers and "pick up lines" are two very different things. Pick up lines are cheesy and do nothing but let her know you want to sleep with her (which, trust me, she already knows), while openers get her into a conversation where you can start building attraction.

- The average attractive woman likely hears dozens of pick up related lines every day. Her defenses are automatically up, and she's learned to reflexively deflect our advances.

- Rehearse a few openers to overcome "stage fright."

- There are two kinds of openers: Direct and indirect. Direct is when you don't hide your intention to pick her up. You use indirect openers to elude her Bitch Shield and get her into a conversation.

- Don't ask yes or no questions. A question, like "Can I buy you a drink?" just gives her the opportunity to say no.

- Opinion openers work like chick crack because they allow women to do two of their favorite things: Give you their opinions and solve someone else's problems. "Cocky and funny" openers position you as a strong, confident man and take the "egomaniac" edge off with humor. They are surprisingly effective with hotter-than-average women.

CHAPTER 6
WEAK POINTS AND STRONG

"Nobody will ever win the battle of the sexes. There's too much fraternizing with the enemy."

—Henry Kissinger

You're standing at the bar with your wingman, and you've successfully used one of your opinion openers on a couple of very hot girls. They are rattling off the pros and cons of dying your hair blonde for your (fictional) daytime talk show appearance, and you and your buddy are fanning the conversational flames. Things are going great—until the whole "dying your hair blonde" discussion is exhausted and the flames start to die down. This will happen every time you open, sometimes within just a few minutes.

Now, she's staring at you with her "Is that all you've got?" look, so you fall back on what you know, and get dragged into the small talk thing. "So, um, where are you from?" "What do you do?" Now she's bored, because you're no more fun or exciting than every other chump who has approached her tonight. It's this point where most guys get the "Well, it was nice meeting you . . ." brush off, right before she turns back to her friends. You shuffle away, chalking up another failed mission.

79

Sun Tzu says, "That your army may be like a grindstone dashed against an egg, use the science of weak points and strong." You don't want to be dashing any eggs with a stone in a bar, but you can be successful by not only finding and exploiting your target's weaknesses, but by also turning what other guys perceive as weak points into strong points. Remember, any idiot in a popped collar can memorize an opener and get pretty good at using it to get women talking. It's what happens *after* that first contact that's important. You can't build a relationship—or even a one night stand—around "Should you floss before or after you brush?" or "I'm tired of you staring at my ass." (Well, technically you could, but would you want to?) At some point you're going to have to *transition* from your opener into real conversation, which is where you're going to continue to show her how entertaining and engaging you are and keep that attraction building. The good news is that transitioning to a real conversation isn't as tricky or difficult as you think—and, even better, small talk doesn't have to be boring.

TELL A GOOD TALE

Remember back in Chapter 3 when we were talking about Mental Strength and I mentioned how women love romance novels? How they are drawn to the highly detailed stories full of compelling characters? Women have a weak spot for a really juicy story. They love rich visuals. They love fully drawn characters. They love to be transported to a fantasy world. They just can't resist. As Sun Tzu says, "You may advance and be absolutely irresistible if you make for the enemy's weak points." And as long as you keep some key things in mind, she'll find you absolutely irresistible, too.

Transitioning from the lull in your opening conversation is as easy as saying something like, "That's so true. And it reminds of the time I went body surfing in Maui with this 300-pound dude wearing a banana hammock . . . well, he *started out* wearing a banana hammock, but then . . ." and launching into it from there. You're off the opener and into a story. She won't care what the story's about as long as she's caught up in the details.

And notice how I started that story. From just those few details, wouldn't you want to hear the rest of it? I could have said, "Hey, I went body surfing once. Have you ever been?" but even I don't want to hear the rest of that. It sounds like you're going to fill some conversational down time with boring stories of some vacation you took years ago. I'd rather donate blood than sit through that. By giving details—Maui, 300-pound dude, a banana hammock that may or may not fall off at some point—you draw her in and get her invested in the story. But as guys, we're not used to going into detail.

Imagine you're telling a story to your buddies about a coworker tripping over a chair in the conference room and hitting the deck right at the beginning of a huge client meeting. It would probably go something like this: "So we're all sitting there, and that geek from accounting comes in carrying a huge stack of papers. He doesn't see that the client has his feet out, so he nails one and goes flying. Papers everywhere. I'm pretty sure he even pissed himself a little. Dude, it was epic." Then you clink the necks of your beer bottles together and laugh your asses off. Story over. The punch line is: geek falls down, important papers are strewn all over, geek is publicly humiliated. That's all we need to know to laugh like a nine-year-old at Chuck E. Cheese.

Women, on the other hand, wouldn't get that at all. Why? Because they need to know the *characters* involved. Only then can they get into the story and see the humor. "Geek falls down" isn't funny all by itself but, "Bernie Bertleman (yeah, that's his real name) is a guy from accounting who *always* wears this ridiculous cardigan sweater and horn rimmed glasses and probably hasn't washed his hair since Star Trek went off the air. He treats the rest of us like we don't have the brains to climb out of a wet paper bag. Well, he comes waltzing into this incredibly important meeting with an incredibly self-important client, Mr. Dumass, who has no sense of humor at all, and once even threw . . ." you get the idea. Only when women know the characters and the details and the circumstances and everything else do they get involved in the story.

So Rule Number One of great storytelling is "Include Details," but hit her with only the relevant details. Keep it tight; don't go wandering off on a tangent. Give her the visuals. Paint a picture for her with words, so she can *see* what you're saying. Pretend you are unspooling a roll of film into a movie projector in her head. And the star of that movie? You.

YOU ARE THE MAIN CHARACTER

Rule Number Two is, "You are the Main Character in the Stories You Tell." Even if the story revolves around a friend, coworker, or someone else, you want to make sure that you focus on how integral *you* are to the story. Why? Because by doing this, you show her that you are an interesting and fun guy who lives an exciting life she definitely needs to be a part of. You are also building attraction by demonstrating strength, loyalty, and fearlessness. And because you know how hooked into the characters she gets, you want her to connect with the most important character: you.

FEEL FREE TO BRAG

This brings us to Rule Number Three: "Brag, but Brag Subtly." If you don't understand why you're bragging, see Rule Number Two. This is your shot to set yourself apart from all the other guys who tried to get her number tonight. You have her attention, you're entertaining, she's hanging on your every word, and it's the perfect time to take advantage and build your value. Just don't go overboard, because there's a fine line you don't want to cross. Just like you can cross over quickly from Entertaining Guy to Dancing Monkey, you can go from a fun guy who tells great stories to a name-dropping, bragging, douchebag, in the blink of an eye.

If you want . . .	You're a Storyteller if . . .	You're a Bragging Douchebag if . . .
. . . to let her know you're athletic.	You say "Last summer a bunch of us were on our yearly mountain bike outing in Moab, when this guy shows up wearing bright Pink Spandex." with strategically placed dramatic pauses.	You say, "So I'm on this softball team and we make it to the state finals, like, every year. We're down one run and I'm batting in the ninth, and the pitcher is shaking because I'm . . . ."
. . . to let her know you have social strength and are a risk taker.	You say, "So me and Big Brad decide to sneak into this *huge* celebrity pool party at Club Bango, and we cut through this random cabana when the security guard wasn't looking. We end up bumping right into Mark Sanchez, the star quarterback for the NY Jets. Knocked a tray of Piña Coladas right out of his hands. Turns out *it's his cabana,* and rather than rat us out and have us tossed out on our asses, he starts mixing us drinks, and invites us to . . ."	You say, "Yeah, I know Mark Sanchez. He's the quarterback of the Jets, you know. Met him at this pool party I was invited to that was exclusively for star athletes. We hung out, he's my boy . . ."

If you want . . .	You're a Storyteller if . . .	You're a Bragging Douchebag if . . .
. . . to show her how loyal you are	You say, "Anyway, I turn around and my boy Frankie D is surrounded by this gang of like fifteen or twenty angry, mean looking sorority girls. *Really* angry sorority girls! And I swear they started putting their hair up in pony tails and looked like they were getting ready to tear him into bite-size pieces. Now I'm a lover, not a fighter, but I have to admit, those Kappa Kappa Kappas were pretty scary. I wasn't going to let Frankie go down alone, so I jump in the middle of them and all hell breaks loose . . ."	You say, "Now, I'm not afraid to throw down when I have to. I mean, my boys know, if someone looks at them funny, I'll be the first one to crack open a skull . . ."

Does this mean you have to have a dozen stories packed away in your brain, ready to pull out at a moment's notice? Not at all. If you have them, great. But a couple of really entertaining or funny or interesting stories that you tell skillfully with great delivery are all you need to transition from your opener. Just make sure that you're the main character, that you make your stories fun and visual, and that you fill them with details. Then great stories will become one of your strongest strong points. And listen, she's never met you. I'm not saying you can flat out make up stories—because you shouldn't— but add in some embellishments here and there? Absolutely.

SMALL TALK DOESN'T HAVE TO BE SMALL

Eventually, after you've told all your stories, the conversation will start to slow down. It's inevitable. And it's the time that guys hate the most—when a woman falls back on what she knows: small talk. It doesn't matter if you're meeting for the first time in a bar, on a date, or even if you've known each other for a little while— women love that inane, mind-melting blather where she asks "So what do you do?" or "Where are you from?" or any of a number of hackneyed, routine, almost robotic questions that people ask each other when they first meet, and they've run out of things to say. Small talk usually signals the end of the excitement; but it doesn't have to. Especially if you keep two things in mind:

1. Women have a need for detail. We went over this when we talked about storytelling, but it's true here too. They need to know details about the people in their lives. This is just part of their getting-to-know-you period.

2. If she's still talking to you, even if it's just small talk, you have the opportunity to keep things fun, build attraction, set yourself apart, and amp up the sexual tension. We may look at it like an interrogation and as though we're being tested—because to a certain degree we are—but think of it this way: If she didn't give a shit about you, she'd just say "thanks" and walk away rather than continuing to pry for more info. So take what most consider the weakest of weak points and turn it into a strong advantage.

KEEP IT OPEN-ENDED

Here's a quick tip before we get into the advanced stuff: When you get pulled into a small talk conversation, always try to ask open-ended questions rather than closed-ended questions. Here's what I mean: If, after she tells you that she's a school teacher, you follow with the usual closed-ended, "So do you like it?" you run the risk of just getting a conversation killing "Yeah, it's okay." Now you have to come up with another question, and your conversation limps along made up of poorly stitched together short questions and answers— one of the main reasons everyone hates small talk. Instead, ask her an open-ended question like, "So if you were trying to talk me into becoming a teacher, give me your Top 5 Reasons Why it's the Best Job in the World." She'll have to think rather than just spit out a yes or no, and you can take any one of her answers and go off into a completely new direction. Think of open-ended questions as the Jaws of Life of your conversational rescue tools. But if you really want to have some fun when the talk turns to small, just lie your ass off . . .

LIE YOUR ASS OFF

When she asks you what you do for a living, who says you have to give her a straight answer? *Average* guys do that. They think their answer has to impress her. "Oh, well I'm a partner in a prestigious firm that . . ." Who gives a shit? Not her. Why, then, are we so compelled to give an honest answer when a woman asks us what we do? Forget that. You want to take advantage of weak points and crush them with your strength—and your strength is being entertaining, having fun, and setting yourself apart from every other Average Frustrated Chump she's ever asked that question to. So have fun with it. *A lot of fun.* (I'll even show you how to take a small talk staple, "So what do you do for a living?" and turn it into an invaluable Shit Test of your own, in Chapter 8.)

Honestly, besides being a minor Shit Test, small talk is really just conversational spackle, there to fill in the gaps and spaces until you can find your way back to real conversation. You know when people ask you how you're doing or how your day was they don't really want or expect an honest answer. You also know that you rarely ever give one. Usually a polite "Fine, how are you?" and then you move on. Treat small talk the same way, and feel free to lie your ass off.

And you don't have to start lying right off the bat. You can also just let the small talk start off as it normally does. Give her the same old boring answers she usually gets for "what do you do?", "where are you from?", etc. Then, when she asks what you like to do for fun (which she will, because women use this to get an idea of what they'll be doing with you should this whole first date thing work out), you can catch her off guard with something completely outrageous. Like telling her you're an internationally renowned Lintist. What's a "Lintist?" Well, you go around to laundromats around town and take the lint out of all the dryers. Then you head out to the studio you built behind your garage and, using nothing but that dryer lint (and never dust bunnies, because you never know what you'll find in those), masterfully create life-size reproductions of great works of art, which you then sell at craft shows and flea markets around the country. Beats the shit out of "I like to go mountain biking," right? Plus, from there you can take the conversation a million different directions, without getting stuck in the small-talk trap.

You can even turn small talk around on her too. Instead of asking her what she does, the expected follow up to her asking you what you do, ask her if she makes a ton of money at her job because, leading immediately into your Lintist story, you need a wealthy sugar mama to support your starving-artist lifestyle. Not this "kinda rich" crap; you need someone who's got the coin to fly you to Europe regularly so you can get the really high quality dryer lint that your discriminating collectors require. Then see if she plays along, and sees the humor in it. (This is where you start to "qualify" her, and see if she's the kind of girl you want to date. Think of it as your own Guy Shit Test. I'll explain in more detail in Chapter 7.)

TAKE A RIDE DOWN THE SEXUAL HIGHWAY

Another way to leverage weak small talk into a strong advantage is to use it to dial up the sexual tension. You're trying to build attraction, so there's nothing wrong with taking the conversation and steering right down the sexual highway. We're guys; we can find the innuendo in anything. Ask her where she's from, and regardless of what she answers, follow with "Oh, you're one of *those* girls . . . I've heard about you . . . I'm going to have to watch myself . . ." and play it up. For another example, you can ask her if she has any pets. Her answer doesn't matter. You follow with, "Really? I have a dog. Wow, that sucks, because you know we'll never end up together. I read a study the other day that said that when a guy with a dog gets together with a girl with a cat/dog/goldfish/no pet, the relationship never lasts. But they did say the sex was incredible while it lasted . . ."

You'd be surprised how receptive women are when you start down the sex path. Most of the time, they enjoy the flirting and go right along with it.

WAR STORY: BOBBY MADE A FRIEND, THE OTHER GUY GOT LAID

This is a story my friend Bobby Rio tells in a short report, "Small Talk Tactics," he wrote on turning up the sexy in ordinary conversation (get a free copy at *www.MakeSmallTalkSexy.com*). It perfectly illustrates how important it is to turn the weakness of seemingly innocent small talk into the strong point of building attraction.

It happened when Bobby was at a fraternity party and saw a really cute girl eating something in the kitchen. He wanted to meet her, so he opened with something cocky/funny about how she must be hungry to be eating over the sink in a dirty frat house. She answered that she came straight from work and needed to eat something before drinking. Bobby had successfully opened her. He asked what she was eating, and it turns out it was some organic health nut bar. Being a health nut himself, Bobby launched into a discussion on health food, figuring this was the perfect way to build rapport and keep her talking.

During the conversation, he discovered they had a common interest: a health guru with a cult-like following. They both happen to have drank the Kool-Aid, and were avid followers. They spent the next hour talking about the guy, his books, beliefs, recipes, everything and anything Bobby can think of to keep the conversation flowing. They even decide to go to see the guy together someday.

By this point Bobby is ecstatic. He's met a great girl who is beautiful, intelligent, fun, health conscious, and they've been talking for hours about a common interest. He's in; this is his next girlfriend, he can feel it. So when she excuses herself to go to the bathroom, he scrambles to find a buddy who can spare a condom. He found one, put it in his pocket, and waited for his "soul mate" to come back.

Only she didn't come back. Walking up the stairs, he saw her talking to one of his frat brothers; a guy who was, in Bobby's words, "an alcoholic, drug-using, wiseass." Figuring his frat brother would just laugh off her health nut ways and eventually piss her off, Bobby guessed she'd only be a few more minutes. He went back down and waited for her. And waited. Until another twenty minutes or so went by.

He went back upstairs and heard them talking in his frat brother's room. Peeking in, he saw his buddy's pants around his ankles, and the girl of his dreams kneeling down in front of him, giving him a hand job. If that wasn't soul crushing enough, she looked up at Bobby, and gave him a look that seemed to say,

"You're a really nice guy, but I'm here to party, not talk about health food, loser."

Bobby was stunned. He had got her talking. He was building attraction. He was engaging and passionate about the topic. She seemed to be genuinely interested in what he was saying. And she probably was. But, and this is important, she was probably only interested on an educational/friendship/curiosity level. Why? Because Bobby never injected anything playful or sexy into the conversation. He just latched on to one topic they had in common, and proceeded to beat it to death. He never took into account that the cute, sweet, fun girl he was connecting with was actually a sexual being who was at a party looking for fun and excitement. He also never established sexual intent. To her, Bobby was just a nice guy who liked some of the same stuff she did. Another "friend." (Sound familiar?) Wiseass frat brother, on the other hand, caught her on her way back from the bathroom, saw her for the hot chick she was, and immediately amped up the sexual tension.

So while Bobby got a "health nut buddy" to talk fitness secrets and recipes with, Frat Bro small talked his way into a very happy ending.

The important thing to remember is to not fear the transition from opener to actual conversation. Come up with some great stories, practice the fine art of making small talk fun and interesting—and sexual—and you shouldn't have to worry about running out of interesting things to say that will keep her attention and build that attraction.

And if you take Sun Tzu's advice that "The clever combatant imposes his will on the enemy, but does not allow the enemy's will to be imposed on him," then you'll understand why it's important to keep the conversation going in order to qualify your target—to see if she's really worth your time.

- Openers are great for getting the conversation started, but you need to get good at transitioning into an actual conversation—which isn't as tricky or difficult as you think.
- Make sure to follow the Three Rules of Storytelling:

    1. Include details. Paint pictures for her with words.
    2. Make sure the main character of those stories is *you*.
    3. Brag, but be subtle about it. You can go from a fun guy who tells great stories to a name-dropping, bragging, douchebag, in the blink of an eye.

- Small talk is inevitable; it's what she knows and falls back on. You can take small talk, the weakest of weak points, and turn it into an advantage.
- No one ever said you had to answer small talk questions truthfully. That equals boring and common. Make stuff up. Be interesting, be entertaining, and set yourself apart from the Average Frustrated Chumps. In other words, lie your ass off.
- Use small talk to dial up the sexual tension.

CHAPTER 7
MANEUVERING

"All's fair in love and war."

—Francis Edward Smedley

Sun Tzu warned, "We cannot enter into alliances until we are acquainted with the designs of our neighbors." What he's basically saying is, don't start picking out new curtains with her or let her pack your sports memorabilia into storage until you know what she's all about. You need to figure out whether or not she's right for you—and if she's worthy of you spending the time and effort to get to know her.

This is a tough concept for a lot of guys to wrap their heads around. Most guys figure if a chick is even remotely interested, they'd better take advantage of it. After all, laid is laid right? Wrong. There's a whole lot of crazy floating around out there—drama queens, soul-suckers, energy vampires, she devils, jealous maniacs, baggage handlers, Debbie Downers, material girls, and an endless parade of other assorted full-blown bat-shit nut jobs—all camouflaged in cute little black dresses and peep toe pumps, waiting patiently for unsuspecting suckers to wander into their webs.

Fortunately, there are also millions of beautiful, smart, intelligent, fun women who want to enhance and enrich your life out there as well. So understand that the odds of finding a great girl are very much in your favor. Your objective then, is to *qualify* the women you are meeting, so you end up with the ones who would love to treat you to a nice home cooked meal, not boil bunnies in your kitchen.

DON'T PLAY RUSSIAN ROULETTE WITH YOUR BITS AND PIECES

Just as every woman has her Attraction Fuels, every guy has those specific essential qualities he wants in a woman. And too many of us tend to settle and overlook weak points. Why? Because, a lot of the time, Little Bruno takes over and does our thinking for us—and Little Bruno's feeling is, "Well, she may not be perfect, but as long as she's perfectly willing . . . ." If that's what you're looking for, good for you. No judgment here. If you want to head home with whatever says yes and play a few rounds of Russian Roulette with your irreplaceable man parts, that's your business. Me? I have standards. And all kidding aside, they are pretty high. At least they are now. I went through the same phase every guy goes through: Tag as many trophies as you can. Ignore any red flags if it means scoring—especially if she's hot.

We've all heard the saying "Crazy pussy is the best pussy," and I went through my share of women who put the "fun" in dysfunctional. I told myself that the wild sex and the fact that I had a hot chick on my arm were worth the insanity going on in the relationship, until I realized that the reason I was stuck in these situations was not because I wanted to be, but because I didn't have any standards. I didn't "acquaint myself with their designs" before entering into an alliance. I didn't set out with a plan to find the right girl for me, my only plan was to find any girl.

YOU ARE THE PRIZE

To find the right girl, you have to start thinking "attract" and stop thinking "pursue." When you have the mindset that *you are the prize*, a woman will need to prove herself worthy of spending time with you. You are not looking for her approval, she needs to seek yours. And this is not an ego thing or a "men are better than women" thing, this is a positive attitude thing that will help you stop bowing down to women (which they hate), and help you attract the type of women you want to *be* with, instead of just sleep with.

See, there's a subtle (and oftentimes not so subtle), power play going on here. Keep in mind that, no matter what, Sun Tzu always recommends fighting from a position of strength. You have to do the same. You must display a higher value than the woman you're trying to attract. Men, especially if they think they're going to get laid, will settle. Women usually won't "date down"; they want to be with a man who is higher up on the social scale than they are.

So, Nice Guys, pay close attention: You need to have the attitude that sex, or the chance of impending sex, is no big deal. I know it may be hard to control your excitement—especially when you're coming off a dry spell that makes Death Valley look like a tropical rain forest—but you need to act like you've been there before and keep a nonchalant attitude. No running over to your boys to tell them the good news. No high fives or fist bumps. (Actually, high fives or fist bumps are pretty much off limits in any situation.) A woman wants a strong, high-value man, not an overly excited thirteen year-old who just had his first make out session at sleep away camp.

Women interpret men's desperation to seek their approval as something associated with those men having lower social value. After all, if you were really cooler than her, you wouldn't need to get her approval, right? The second you start appearing complacent or needy, she's turned off. She wants a man, not a Moodle. (A Man Poodle, mentioned in *She's Outta My League*. Not a bad movie to watch to prove how higher value trumps all else.) So, man up and don't let her "out Alpha" you.

DON'T TAKE THE BAIT

Sun Tzu says, "Do not swallow a bait offered by the enemy." Remember those Shit Tests she keeps throwing at you? A big part of why she tests you is because she's trying to get you to reveal your lower value by falling for them. She wants to see if you'll try to prove your worth or show any neediness by constantly agreeing with her—or, worse, see how hard you work to prove that you're worthy of the honor of having sex with her These things will instantly lower your value in her eyes, but most of us do them instinctively every time we interact with women. Time to stop swallowing that bait. Things will change for you forever when you fully realize and believe that your value comes from within you. And this doesn't just go for meeting women, but for life in general.

YOU CAN'T HIT THE BULL'S-EYE WHEN YOU DON'T HAVE A TARGET

Just as you need to know your goals in order to achieve them, just as you need to have a target in order to hit it, when you know what you're looking for—and not looking for—in a woman, the chance of you finding the one who is right for you, increases dramatically. So what do you want?

BUILD A WISH LIST

Grab a pen and some paper and make a list of the core, positive qualities you're looking for in your ideal woman. It shouldn't be an exhaustive list—after all, the world only has so many PhDs who can name every year the Yankees won the World Series, run a four-minute mile, and quote every line from *The Hangover*. You want to list the important qualities that would really make you happy.

Stuck? Here are some things you may be looking for in your ideal woman:

* Intelligent
* Athletic
* Adventurous/Risk Taker
* Fun Loving
* Witty/Sarcastic
* Great Sense of Humor
* Creative
* Self-Reliant
* Gregarious / Friendly
* Emotionally Strong
* Optimistic
* Confident
* Successful
* Driven
* Family-Oriented/Mom Material
* Sophisticated

You get the idea. What you're doing is building your wish list of the ideal girl for you, what you'd ask Santa for if he could stuff her in your stocking. And while I didn't include any physical or sexual qualities above, feel free to do that on your own list.

DEAL BREAKERS

You also need to list the qualities that you are *not* looking for, i.e., the deal breakers. These should be the things we tend to overlook when there's great sex involved—or even the potential for great sex. Men tend to stay in some bad relationships way longer than we should thanks to what goes on behind closed doors, so check for deal breakers before you get lured in by the promise of kick ass hook ups and, if you find any, be sure to get out while all your favorite parts are still attached. Here are some Deal Breaker Qualities to Look Out For Before You Get Hooked:

- Jealous
- Negativity/Bitterness
- Bitchy
- Doesn't Have a Lot of Friends (Especially Female Friends)
- Drama Queen
- Pessimistic
- Needy
- Lazy
- "Stage 5 Clinger"
- Has Tons of Baggage
- Moody
- Materialistic
- Flaky/Unreliable
- Drug User
- Attention Whore

Pay close attention to these because, when men are out in the field in the heat of battle, sometimes we tend to focus on looking for the good while the bad eludes us. For me, all bets are off if I meet girl who has even one of these qualities. I can deal with a woman who only has a few of my ideal qualities—and is maybe missing one or two of the important ones—but I'm out if she's bitchy or negative or needy. There are just too many fish in the sea to settle for one that's spoiled. You must have this mindset too; once you do, it'll start to come across when you meet women. The desperation, the need to make every girl you meet "like" you, and the need to prove yourself to her will fade away. As a result, your interactions will become more relaxed, you won't seem needy, and she'll start to see you as having higher value; she'll even start trying to prove herself to you.

MAKE HER PROVE HERSELF

Look at celebrities and rock stars. Do they ever act needy and desperate when around women? Of course not. By nature of their position and achievements they possess a much higher value, and women are constantly trying to qualify themselves or prove that they are worthy to be with them. Do you have to be an actual rock star to score women like one? Nope. All you have to do is demonstrate the value of a rock star, which means understanding that there will always be an endless supply of qualified women for you to meet and attract. There's no need to "settle" or suffer from "One-itis," another term coined by Mystery that describes the debilitating disease guys get when they feel the woman they have met is the one-and-only girl for them and therefore don't realize there are thousands of other women out there who fit their desires.

And again, you have to accept that this has nothing to do with looks. It has everything to do with attitude and belief of value. For confirmation, just look at all the less-than-classically good look-ing guys out there, celebrities and rock stars included, who regu-larly score hot chicks. They get them and keep them because of their attitude, character, and sense of high value.

So should you start to qualify a woman right from the min-ute you meet her? No. There's no need to try to sway her if she's clearly not interested. At that point it's best to eject and move on to another target. How can you tell if she's interested? Look at her body language: Is she playing with her hair? Primping or fixing her clothes? Looking longingly into your eyes, or touching you a lot? Playing along enthusiastically with your small talk games? Even giving you Shit Tests can be an indicator. But once you get some indication that she's interested, feel free to make her work for you attention.

SHIT TEST REDUX

One way to qualify a woman is to give her your own Guy Shit Test. Ask her some questions or tell her a story and see how she reacts; tease her when she doesn't answer the way you want. This is one of the reasons that the cocky and funny approach works; you display a higher value when you make fun of her. Most women have never experienced this; they have lived their entire lives as the "selector" never having been the "selectee" and it throws them off their defenses, which lets you see who they really are.

Here's my own personal qualifying Shit Test: When a woman would fall back on small talk and ask me what I do for a living, I used to answer honestly: I'm a men's lifestyle writer. This led to, "Oh, that's interesting. What do you write about?" I'd tell her, and then we'd ping pong back and forth for a while; she'd pretend to be interested and nod politely, but even though I do get to go on a lot of cool trips and meet some semi-famous people, writing is mostly a lonely business—and it's not very exciting.

So I started to make stuff up. And I ended up qualifying women by accident. (Remember how in Chapter 6 I showed how lying your ass off in a humorous way can help you open a woman? Well, it works for qualifying too.) So, when they asked me what I did for a living, I answered that I had kiosks at malls all over the country where I repair and service disposable lighters: I refill them. Change out flints. Adjust the flame. Whatever the customer wants. Usually for about $2 or $3 dollars each. So with the high demand and large volume I do pretty well and make a comfortable living.

I really started making stuff up out of boredom, and because I didn't want to go through the whole, "I'm a writer"/"Oh really, what so you write?" crap. But what I found was that I'd get one of three responses whenever I told this ridiculous story:

1. The chick would stare at me, seriously confused, and kind of go, "Huh? Can you really fix a disposable lighter? I didn't know that." Or just say, "I'm not really sure how that works. Why would you fix something you can just throw away. I'm confused."

2. She would say something like "Well that's just stupid. Who would pay $3 to fix a $1 disposable lighter? That's why they call them 'disposable.'" Some women even get a little angry with me for even trying to pull that off on them.

3. She would totally play along and start role playing with me, jokingly asking questions about services I provide, and suggesting we should go into business refilling disposable pens.

When I got those answers, I immediately knew which women I was after; the women who responded one of the first two ways, were definitely not my type. Number 1 is out because I need a girl who is sharp and "gets it" when I'm being sarcastic or funny. Number 2 is out because she obviously has zero sense of humor, and that's important to me; I'm also not down with dating chicks that set off my Bitch-O-Meter that quickly. The women who fell into number 3 tended to be fun and adventurous, loved to play, had great senses of humor, were willing to be silly, and were obviously quick witted. All major qualities I look for so, within just a few minutes of meeting someone, I was able to qualify her and know if I wanted to continue the conversation or not. Because why stick around, trying to prove myself to a Number 2 girl, when somewhere, in that crowd, a Number 3 was waiting to have some fun?

MALLS ARE FOR MORE THAN JUST SHOPPING

Another example of qualifying right from the opener is the shopping mall opener dreamed up by pick up artist and dating coach Tyler Durden. The technique is explained in *The Full Guide to Being Cocky and Funny* by Old Flirty Bastard. It shows how you can open, get signs of attraction, and qualify almost all at the same time. It goes like this: Say you see a hot babe shopping in a mall store. Grab a really ugly or ridiculous looking shirt off the rack and say to her "Whoa, this is sweet! I should try this on right now . . . come on, check this out." Start moving over to a mirror, hopefully with her following you. (If she does, that's your first sign there's some interest.) As you head to the mirror, grab another one of the same ugly/ridiculous shirts for her. Have her put it on and stand in front of the mirror with your arm around her like you're posing for a picture. Then say "We should steal these!" and watch her reaction. If she starts plotting along with you—in on the joke and going with it—you know you have a girl with the fun, playful quality you're looking for. If she says no, grab the stuff in her cart and make like you're running out the door with it. If she starts to play along now, she qualifies. If she gets mad, annoyed, or calls for security . . . well, she's not for you.

KEEP THE QUESTIONS COMING

You can also qualify her by asking direct questions once she's been opened and you're in a conversation. At that point, it's perfectly okay to ask, "So, are you adventurous?", or "Tell me the most creative thing you've done lately." This way you start walking her down the path of proving herself to you.

Keep in mind you want to stay away from straying into small talk. "Where are you from?" doesn't even keep the conversation alive and interesting, let alone help qualify. You want to ask questions that give you insight into who she is as a person, and let you know if she has the qualities on your Wish List. In Durden's shopping mall example, he's looking for a girl who is playful and adventurous. (And possibly a little bit of a bad girl.) She doesn't play along, he moves along. Simple as that.

Let's say you use the line above, "Tell me the most creative thing you've done lately" and she responds with, "Creative? I don't know. Does shopping for shoes count as creative?" Well you know right away she's not creative at all. And if that's an important quality on your list, you can disqualify her right now.

So go to your Wish List and pick out a couple of the qualities that are most important to you. Then come up with some qualifying questions that'll give you a clear signal whether to keep moving forward, or hit the eject button and spend your time looking elsewhere.

KEEP IT COCKY. AND FUNNY.

The ever-popular cocky and funny qualifiers are another incredibly effective way to get a woman—especially a really hot one—to try to prove her worth to you. They work precisely because she is so used to hearing words of praise come out of the mouths of every guy who talks to her that, when you say something like, "Oh look, your nose wiggles when you talk. That's soooo adorable," she gets thrown a little and wonders why *you* aren't trying to prove yourself to *her*. How dare you point out an imperfection? Don't you, like every other lowly male of the species, realize what a goddess she is? The (implied) answer is "no."

You are giving her compliments tinged with a hint of negativity, which is why pickup artists call them "Negs." (Remember we first talked about Negs in Chapter 3?) "I like your nails. Are they real?" "I bet you're even more beautiful without all that makeup you have on." Negs show a woman that you're not impressed; that you talk to incredibly beautiful women all the time and, in fact, she's not even the hottest woman you've chatted with that day. You want to give the impression that you're a man of high value who is always around beautiful women—and she needs to prove why she should be included in that exclusive club.

This was the hardest concept for me to accept, but when I let go and tried it the results were amazing. When I stopped pursuing and worshipping, I found the response was not "well screw you then, I'm going to find a guy who will chase me." It was "Why aren't you chasing me? Look at how incredible I am." A word of advice though: Keep your qualifying obvious—you want her to know she needs to prove herself to you—but don't be invasive or overly intimidating. You want to qualify her, not make it impossible for her to do so or prove that she's worthy.

LEAVE THE ESCAPE HATCH OPEN

Sun Tzu says, when maneuvering against an opponent, never make them feel as if they are surrounded or trapped. "When you surround an enemy," he wrote, "leave an outlet free. This does not mean that the enemy is to be allowed to escape. The object is to make them believe that there is a road to safety, and thus prevent their fighting with the courage of despair. For you should not press a desperate foe too hard." So if the girl you're qualifying starts to feel like this is an exam or an interrogation—or an impossible test to pass—she may become insulted or offended and, rather than try to prove herself, begin to fight back. And this can turn nasty.

For example, if you like tall women, but you're talking to a girl who is short, telling her "I don't like short women," isn't qualifying. It's letting her know that you consider something she can't do anything about to be a negative and a deal breaker. Not smart. You're not giving her "a road to safety," you're causing her to feel insulted and attacked. Instead, stick to things that she can control so she always has a way to qualify herself to you. This also leaves "an outlet free" in case she decides not to prove herself to you. For example, saying "I love women with a great sense of humor" allows her to show you she can appreciate a joke.

What happens if you do go too far and she starts to get justifiably angry? Be a man and apologize. Just do it without losing value. Don't say "Oh, I'm so sorry. I'm just a dick. Sometimes I forget where to draw the line . . . ." Instead say that you had older sisters (or cousins, or neighbors) growing up, teasing was all part of how you interacted, and it comes out sometimes when you start feeling comfortable around a woman.

WAR STORY: She Wanted My Hat . . . She Got the Boot

I was at a sports bar one Saturday afternoon to watch a big college football game with a group of buddies. There was this incredibly hot girl there who was dressed like she was about to shoot some sort of sports porn: super short shorts, knee-high striped socks, and a football "jersey" that was so cut up and cropped, it was basically a pair of numbers held together by strips of pink fabric. So, yeah, she was there to watch the game.

So this chick was bouncing from table to table, guy to guy, just sucking in all the attention she can get. Dudes are buying her drinks, offering her their seats, their laps, their French fries . . . anything and everything she wants, in an attempt to get her to "like" them. Immediately I see her as a classic Attention Whore.

After working the room for a while, she bounces her way over to our table and does her whole "Oh, you guys look cool, I think I'll hang out with you for a while . . . can I have a beer?" routine. And of course my buddy is eager to hand her a cold one. You could literally see his value deflating.

That day I was wearing one of my favorite baseball caps. It looks like it's covered in a regular camouflage design, but when you look closely, you see that the camo "blobs" are actually made out of the silhouettes of naked women. It's unique, and always gets a reaction when people realize what it is. Women especially have strong reactions, which is why I like to wear it. (Remember "peacocking" from Chapter 3?) So Sports Porn Chick sees the hat, notices that it's covered in naked ladies, and makes a beeline for it and says, "I love your hat." Then, grabbing at it, she declares, "I want it."

"Whoa, whoa, whoa!" I say snatching her arm and leaning back. "That's my favorite hat. And I'm not giving it up."

"But I said I want it." Bats eyelashes, tries to look extra pouty. (Another quality I hate: Fake Baby Talk with a side order of You Made Me Sad.)

"I don't care. You want it, you gotta earn it."

She looked at me with that "How dare you" look, and stormed off to find some other sap who would give her whatever she asked for.

I wish I could tell you that I was showing Strength of Character, defusing her Shit Tests, Demonstrating Higher Value, blowing her off because of Deal Breaker Qualities, etc. But truth be told, I just didn't want this chick to have my favorite hat. But here's what happened: When we were leaving at the end of the game, she came up to me and said if I ever decided to give up the hat, to call her. She then pressed her phone number into my hand, smiled, and left.

Was I the best looking guy in the bar that day? Not even close. Was I the richest? Not by a long shot. But I was probably the only guy in the bar who passed her Shit Tests and showed her that I had much higher value than she did, which got me the most desired digits in there that day.

. . . And by the way, if you're waiting for me to say I called her and we got together and made a sports porn of our own, you'll be waiting a long time. I absolutely did not call her. She just about nailed a perfect score on my Deal Breaker List. Highest total ever. One giant walking red flag. And I learned the hard way to steer very clear of those.

Make sure to make your list of what you want in an ideal woman part of your early battle planning—and don't ever be afraid to make the girls you meet qualify themselves. Women do it to us all the time, and they have no fear of walking away if we aren't what they are looking for. They instinctively believe that they are a prize worth fighting for, and there will always be a flood of other guys available who do qualify. It's time for us to feel the same way.

But that's not to say that things will always go smoothly, even if you do have your battle plan all laid out. Sometimes you have to resort to some fancy verbal footwork . . . so keep reading.

- Do not enter into an alliance with a woman until you are acquainted with her "designs."
- You have to know exactly the type of woman you want, the qualities she has, and the qualities that are deal breakers. There are millions of women out there who fit the qualities you're looking for.
- You have to understand that you have high value and that you are a prize to be sought in your own right. So don't pursue; attract.
- Don't settle. And don't catch "One-itis" thinking the one you're talking to is the one and only.
- Know that there's a subtle "value" power play going on. Women won't date a guy they perceive to be of lower value, and they'll put you through a variety of Shit Tests to challenge your value
- You don't have to be a celebrity or rock star to attract women like one.
- When it comes to sex, play it like you've been there before. No high fiving or fist-pumping your buddies.
- Qualifying takes place after there is attraction, but some tactics let you know right from the get-go if she's worth your time. Use Guy Shit Tests, direct questions, and be cocky and funny to get her to prove that she's worthy to you.
- Never make a woman feel as though she's trapped or make it impossible for her to qualify to you. Don't "Neg" her for things she can't change, like her height.

CHAPTER 8
VARIATION OF TACTICS

"Love is the ultimate outlaw. It just won't adhere to any rules. The most any of us can do is to sign on as its accomplice."

—Tom Robbins

Okay; bubble bursting time. Just as in actual battle, sometimes things don't go according to plan. Everything you do is not going to work every time no matter how well planned, how often you practice, or how perfect your delivery is. Openers don't work 100 percent of the time. And there's always the chance that the woman you've approached is having issues—a recent breakup, bad day at work, cramps, whatever—that she decides to take out on you when you come up with your story about dryer lint art. It happens. Even Sun Tzu didn't win 100 percent of his battles. (But don't tell him I told you. He's very sensitive about that.)

You have to be able to adapt to any situation and know what kind of situation you're in. After all, there's a big difference between a Bitch Shield and a bitch. And there are a variety of land mines you can step on and any number of grenades that may get thrown your way during a mission. You may also run into Cockblockers, Mother Hens, White Knights, Overprotective Family Members, Drunken Morons, and a motley crew of other obstacles you'll need to verbally tap dace around, but I'll talk about these in upcoming chapters. Right now, you just need to deal with the woman you're standing in front of and survive whatever she throws at you. Because if you're not at your totally alert best, you'll get buried.

Sun Tzu advised, "In hemmed-in situations, you must resort to stratagem. In a desperate position, you must fight. There are roads that must not be followed, towns that must not be besieged." When your back is against the wall, you have to think your way out of the tight spot and avoid being led into some verbal back alley that you can't fight your way out of; stay sharp, and you'll be able to save a bad situation. If you find yourself in a position where you have no other choice, fighting is your last resort. (And we are talking about verbal fighting. There's never a situation where tagging a mouthy chick with a right hook is appropriate—no matter what she said about your beloved mother.) There are roads women will try to lead you down, and you're screwed if you're not paying attention and follow along. Finally, you need to learn which towns (read: women) must not be besieged.

You need to have a Plan B, even if you have the ultimate battle plan. Train yourself in verbal Kung Fu so that, no matter what's thrown your way, you can deflect it the same way Bruce Lee shakes off flying side kicks.

TOWNS THAT MUST NOT BE BESIEGED

Let's first take a quick look at the women you should never tangle with, the ones who are looking to shove a verbal Scud Missile up your ass. There are three main categories of Women Who Should Never Be Besieged—but only one is obvious before you are already engaged and her weapons are locked on.

THE ANGRY DRUNK

The Angry Drunk is easy to spot—especially if she's already arguing with her friends, tearing some other poor bastard a new one, or throwing things. I don't care how incredibly hot she is, or if you think she's an easy wild sex target, you need to consider her a No Fly Zone. Give her a wide berth and stay as far away as you can. If it's too late and she spots you, or you didn't realize how shit faced and pissed off she was before you approached, the best you can do is treat her like an unstable explosive. Be very gentle. Agree with whatever she says. Laugh at her jokes and comments about your haircut, and slowly back away. Tell her you have to pee. Tell her your parole officer is waiting outside. Cough and tell her you have the Ebola virus and it's highly contagious. Do whatever you have to do to get away without making her think you're leaving because of something she did. Because if she does, she'll become like Cosmotini-fueled napalm; she'll stick to you and burn you down.

THE ANGRY BITCH

Unless she has a perma-scowl on her face, the Angry Bitch is like a booby-trapped doorway: You'll walk in and she'll blow up before you have a chance to react. It doesn't matter what she's so upset or ticked off about, she's going to take it all out on you. Loudly. Maybe she was fired today, maybe she had a fight with her mother, or maybe she just caught her boyfriend cheating and you're the first guy to approach her since she walked in on him with someone else; all that venom will be directed squarely at you.

Your best bet is to eject quickly and quietly since you don't want to a) Get her even angrier or b) Draw a lot of negative attention your way and ruin your chances with anyone else in the place. It's not advised, but if you feel the need to get a word in before you go, try something like "I'm so sorry, I was looking for the Cute and Cuddly section of the bar, I must have wandered into the Bite My Friggin' Head Off For No Friggin' Reason section by mistake. My apologies." (Who knows, it might make her laugh and drop the nastiness.) But under no circumstances should you *ever* make a comment about what time of the month it must be—unless you want to be spitting out pieces of her Manolo Blahniks for the next three months.

THE MOTHER BEAR

Not to be confused with a Mother Hen, who is just a busybody all up in her friend's business trying to make it difficult for you, the Mother Bear is not playing around when it comes to keeping you away from her cubs (read: friends). And she'll tear your damn fool head off to prove it if you push her.

Why is she so overprotective? No idea. It could be any number of things. Maybe her cub just had her heart broken and the last thing the Mother Bear wants is another asshole man coming on to her. Maybe there's more to their relationship than just being friends. Doesn't matter. This is a situation you do not want to be involved in. All the Mother Bear wants to do is attack, humiliate, and otherwise verbally cut you off at the knees. You have to ask yourself if the cub is worth you traversing her friend's barbwire-laced minefield, knowing that the Mother Bear will hit you with one loud "I said to leave us the fuck alone!" after another and make you look like some sort of clingy stalker to everyone else in the place. Ninety-nine percent of the time, that answer is a big no.

DO SOME VERBAL KUNG FU

In addition to the three fine ladies we've just discussed, you may also run into Cockblockers and Mother Hens—the women, or sometimes even the other guy, who will run interference on your advances and try to make you look stupid so you'll slink away without your target in tow. They'll do this by throwing you curveballs in the form of obnoxious questions, or fastballs at your head in the form of direct insults. How you handle them is the difference between proving your worth and value and marching forward to victory, and going home embarrassed and alone with bullet holes in your ass.

So when do you know to parry and thrust and take on her verbal assault in an attempt to turn it around in your favor? When she breaks out her Shit Test, for one. If you look at what she is doing as a test, instead of a personal attack, you'll fare much better. Men tend to get emotional and angry when attacked and want to fight back, and this is never a good idea. You want to think of her testing you as a chance to engage in witty repartee. And if you don't know what I mean by that, go online and find some clips from *Moonlighting*, the mid-'80s TV show that launched Bruce Willis's career and propelled him to superstardom. The main reason for this is the rapid fire back and forth of the characters played by Willis and Cybill Shepherd. One would throw an insult at the other and get a witty comeback in return; usually it was Cybill tossing the insult and Bruce volleying it back at her with a witty line. Not only did it show Willis's character to be a strong and intelligent guy who didn't put up with anyone's shit, let alone a woman he had a thing for, but it also drove the sexual tension between them through the roof. And you don't have to be a TV character to make that happen.

When she gives you shit, give it right back. The worst thing you can do—and we know this from the failures of Nice Guys, and the deflation of Value—is to let it stick to you. And believe me, shit sticks. So don't accept it and don't apologize for something she accuses you of. Turn whatever she says back around.

For example:

- If she accuses you of being too sexual, tell her she's being too prudish.
- If she asks you to buy her a drink, tell her that will only happen if she gives you a ten-minute neck massage first.
- If she makes fun of the shirt you're wearing, tell her to feel free to take it off you, or ask her to take you shopping so she can buy you a nicer one.
- If she says you're too old/too young, tell her you have plenty of experience/are looking for a woman to show you the ropes.
- If she says you're boring her, let her know that only unintelligent people get bored easily. Did she graduate from high school?
- If she makes fun of your opener and says it was stupid or lame, say "Okay Miss Smartypants, how would you have approached you?"
- If she says you're a dick, reply that that's probably the reason she's having so much fun playing with you.

And so on and so forth. The idea is that you don't internalize or personalize her banter and let her get under your skin. If you do, she wins and you lose—in a big way.

WAR STORY: That Would Never Work on a Real Woman

Besides posting random thoughts and breaking news to my Twitter account every day (Twitter.com/thebachelorguy), I also post links to my blog posts. One day I tweeted a link to an article about how to strike up a conversation with women, aimed at guys who were having trouble approaching. Included in the article was the use of opinion openers, an obvious option for guys who are really scared to talk to women.

A few hours later I was named in an angry tweet from some chick who called bullshit on the entire article. Publicly. She says there is no way she, or any other intelligent woman for that matter, would fall for something as stupid as being asked her opinion for something inane like whether or not they wash a can opener before putting it back in the drawer, in a bar, by a stranger.

So I contacted her and asked her what she meant by "fall for." According to her, that approach would send up red flags; she would immediately know that a guy was trying to hit on her, and she'd clam up and blow him off. She doesn't just "get into" conversations with strangers.

Interesting. Well, who do you get into conversations with? She replied, no one she didn't know. She could never be tricked into having a long conversation with a stranger, especially if his intention was to pick her up. Way too smart for that. Never happen. She'd simply walk away from it. I wrote back that I totally agreed. She seemed far more intelligent than the average girl in a bar. I couldn't see her getting hooked in. Then I asked her for her opinion on what she thought would work on her. What subject would get her talking? Simple small talk? An offer to buy a drink? Personally, she said, she liked the direct approach. For a guy to just come with it and tell her he was interested. That would be his only option since, if he attempted to get her to talk to him using any "tricks," she would see it coming a mile away and simply shoot him down.

I told her I was impressed and that I hadn't met a woman with such a finely tuned Bullshit Meter. I thanked her for setting me straight. And it was right after she said "You're welcome" that I decided it was time to let her off the hook. My next tweet to her read: "But you do realize that you just had a twenty minute convo with a stranger about not getting tricked into a convo with a stranger."

"Um, yeah. You're right." was her final reply.

Now had this been an actual pick up situation, rather than me defending myself on a social media platform, I could have said something like, "This is getting really interesting, and I'd love to hear more of what you have to say. 140 characters isn't cutting it. Give me your email address and we can discuss this properly. In complete sentences." I say the odds were in my favor that she would have given me her email address.

The moral here is to always be on your toes and willing to change course on a dime if the situation warrants it. Knock her off her game with a great comeback, or series of comebacks, and you'll not only increase your value, but the attraction and sexual tension as well. At the very least you'll leave with your dignity—and Value—intact, especially if there was no attraction there to begin with.

But it's not just what you say and how you say it that will have an effect on her reaction. *Where* you approach her will play a big role in your success. There are places that can actually increase your chances of having a victorious mission and you'll get your road map in the next chapter.

- No matter how well laid your plans, sometimes things just don't work out the way you expected. You need to be able to think on your feet, and adapt to any situation, if you're going to come out of this mission successfully.
- Sun Tzu advised resorting to strategy when hemmed in, but warned there are roads that should not be followed, and towns that must not be besieged. The same goes for women. The three types of Women Who Should Never Be Besieged are:

1. The Angry Drunk: Doesn't matter if she's hot and willing, think of her as an unstable explosive. Back away slowly, and don't do anything to set her off.
2. The Angry Bitch: Something got her fired up today, she's looking to take someone's ass home in her purse. And you don't want to be the guy who goes home assless.
3. The Mother Bear: Different than a Mother Hen, who just likes to hover over and look out for her flock, the Mother Bear will unleash her fangs and claws and shred anyone who dares come close to her "cub."

- The ones you are free to engage are Shit Testers, Cockblockers, and Mother Hens. Look at what they are throwing at you as a test, not a personal attack; a chance for you to engage in witty repartee.
- Take what she throws at you and don't accept or apologize for it. Instead, turn it back around on her.

CHAPTER 9

THE ARMY ON THE MARCH

"Beware of pretty girls in dance halls and parks who may be spies—as well as bicycles, revolvers, uniforms, arms, dead horses, and men lying on roads— they are not there accidentally."

—From a Soviet infantry manual, issued in the 1930s

Sun Tzu could tell a lot about his enemies just by the places they camped and how they kept their camps. He knew which locations offered the best cover for hiding. He knew that the sudden rising of birds meant an ambush was coming on the spot below. He studied the way dust rose from the ground to tell if he would face a rush of chariots, or an infantry. If his enemies were restless and shouting at night, he knew they were fearful. He knew that they were ready to fight to the death just from the fact that they failed to hang their cooking pots over the fire. All of this info came from simply knowing where his enemies were and how they looked. It's the same in dating. Where you meet a woman can say a lot about her, and at the same time your grooming habits and what your place looks like when she comes over can give her a world of information about you. So let's take a look at both.

GO WHERE THE WOMEN ARE

Now that you know the basics of what to do when you meet a woman, you're probably thinking, "Okay, but where do I go to actually meet them?" Good question. And the answer is "You go where the women are." Before you say, "Screw you, Captain Obvious," look at that answer closely. Notice how all throughout this book I've been saying "bar" or "club" with the occasional "mall" thrown in when talking about where you are approaching, opening, and engaging with women? I did that because those are the most common places guys think of when thinking about meeting girls. But they are not necessarily the *best* places to meet them—especially if the women you're interested in aren't the type to be out getting drunk in a smoky bar until 3A.M., which most of the time, if you look at your list of desired qualities, they aren't. So you need to think outside of the bar box.

So I'll say it again: "Go where the women are." And, with the exception of the ladies room, anywhere they can go is where you should be. This means we need to address something first, and that thing is your Geographic Homophobia.

YOU DON'T HAVE TO DRINK WHITE ZINFANDEL TO GO TO AN ART GALLERY

Geographic Homophobia: The fear of being in or anywhere near any place most guys consider "gay." A dance class: gay. A wine mixer at an art gallery: gay. An Asian-fusion cooking class: gay. A class where you learn the art of flower arranging: super gay.

You need to get over thinking that these things are only for chicks and guys who drink white zinfandel and love Broadway shows. Why? Because they are not gay. They may be female-centric, but they are not female only. And because every meatheaded, unevolved, Neanderthal is avoiding these places like the plague, the female-to-male ratio at these things is off the charts. The quality of a woman who is sipping a nice Spanish Rioja at a downtown gallery is going to be way higher than that of one downing Jack and Cokes at the local dive. Plus, there are so many openers that you can use at a wine mixer at an art gallery, your head should be spinning.

THE DANCE OF PASSION COMES BEFORE THE HORIZONTAL MAMBO

The belief that dance classes are just for bored women, their gay best friends, and guys prepping for their wedding day is a hot steaming pile of nonsense. Dance classes are a great place to meet single women, especially when the classes require a lot of touching, like in salsa or tango. Name something sexier than the tango. Yeah, I thought not.

EAT. PRAY. LOVE. I MEAN SCORE.

Ever taken a yoga class? Those classes are wall-to-wall with women in tight outfits, bending in ways you didn't know they could bend. And the majority of them are health nuts. Check the adult education listings or Meetup.com groups. (If you don't know what that is, check them out online. They list thousands of groups in thousands of interest areas, and the members listings are right there for you to check out first.) You'll find opportunities like cooking classes, pottery classes, wine appreciation classes, book clubs—and if your ideal girl is likely to be at one of these events, you'd better be there too. You'll always find women who are intelligent, fun, and looking to better themselves, rather than ones who are just looking to get drunk and hook up. (Not that there's anything wrong with that . . .)

Bottom line, just like Sun Tzu studied the terrain for clues as to where his enemies would be and how to best engage them, you should be studying the terrain around you for clues as to where to find the types of women you want to engage.

A side note: Once you have secured a date, don't be like most guys who feel "date" = coffee or dinner. Remember, you're different. You're exciting. You are going to show her a better time than the other mooks who took her out before you. So how about a fitness date, where you go biking or hiking? Or a gallery date, where you head downtown and stop in all the places on gallery row? Even window shopping at a funky downtown area beats going to the mall for a coffee. And all lend themselves to a flood of conversation way more than sitting across from someone and playing the "Getting to Know You" game.

KEEP UP YOUR CAMP

Now eventually you're going to have a woman come back to your place and there's a possibility it may happen the night you meet. And just like Sun Tzu could tell everything about his enemies by how they kept their camps, how you live says a lot to her about you and who you are. So take a look around. Is your place Date Worthy? Or does it look like a jail cell with nothing on the walls, threadbare furniture, and last week's dishes still in the sink? It had better be a place she feels comfortable in and would want to spend some time. And I'm talking about more than just having clean sheets on the bed and your porn stashed in the closet. (Well, that last part depends on what type of girl is coming over.)

To make sure you're always prepared, here's your Checklist of Things to Do Before She Comes Over:

- ❑ Start clean. At the very least make sure your place is always vacuumed, especially if you have pets. Put the dishes—and everything else—away. Wipe down your kitchen and bathroom counters and make absolutely sure the toilets are spotless. Be sure to have plenty of fresh towels.

- ❑ Have the right props. You need things that show her who you are, and spark conversation. Pictures of friends and family, an interesting piece of art or furniture, books on your coffee table, or even a toy (if it's a vintage or collector's item and not creepy like a little kid's toy) all make great props.

- ❑ Check the thermostat. You know how women are always cold. Hopefully she'll be comfortable enough with you to want to get naked, but that won't happen if it's too cold.

- ❑ Install dimmers. Mood lighting works wonders.

- ❑ Invest in scented candles. They'll help mask manly odors and, in addition, nothing "sets the mood" like candlelight.

- ❑ Speaking of scent, you should always use room deodorizers and those plug-in air fresheners. Potpourri? In moderation. You don't want her getting the wrong idea.

- ❑ Have a full pantry and things to snack on. She's coming over for a movie? Better have popcorn, and not just that stuff that you microwave. Invest in fresh popcorn that you pop yourself. (It's easy and tastes way better. Google how to.) Strawberries? A must. Wine is too, both red and white.

Champagne is even better. Keep a bottle of white wine and champagne in the fridge to make sure they're chilled beforehand.

☐ Make sure there are all necessary ingredients in your pantry for you to make her breakfast the next morning.

☐ Preselect music. Have your iPod loaded with enough mood music to last much longer than you do.

☐ Protection should be a no brainer and, since this is your place, the condoms are your responsibility. Keep them in the nightstand so you're not getting up and running to the bathroom.

☐ Your bed sheets should be clean and fresh, and there should be an extra pillow for her.

☐ Plan ahead for her staying over. It's tricky, but have a new, unopened toothbrush for her. Some women see this as the sign of you being a "player," but there are a number of excuses you can use for having it. For example, you could say you had your six month dental cleaning and they gave it to you or that it's been in the closet for months.

PLAY TO YOUR STRENGTHS

It's your time to shine when she's on your home turf, so think hard: What are you good at? Can you cook a bad-ass salmon dish? Can you mix the meanest margarita this side of the Rio Grande? Even brewing a special coffee drink that you picked up at this little place in Madrid can be impressive. All are great excuses to get her over, and great opportunities to show her how incredible you are.

If you can't think of anything offhand, pick something now, long before you start inviting women over. Look up a recipe for a fish or chicken dish (it should go without saying that anything like ribs or wings is out of the question) or a unique cocktail, and practice it until you can you do it without thinking. You want to be talking with her while you're whipping it up, not concentrating on not burning the fish, so you need to be able to carry this out on autopilot. Do it right, and you'll set yourself apart—and have her asking for a repeat visit.

ARE YOU IN DATE SHAPE?

While we are talking about making sure that your place is in shape, this is a good time to take a look at yourself and make sure *you* are in date shape. And I'm not (necessarily) talking about your spare tire or love handles. I mean the big picture.

While looks may not be as important to women as other things, your grooming is incredibly important. If you're reading this and thinking, "I don't need to change anything, I just need to learn a few canned openers, get women to talk to me and they'll see what a great guy I am. I look just fine in my Three-Wolves-Howling-at-the-Moon shirt and man sandals," then it's time for a wakeup call.

I'll sum it up this way: One time I went to pick up my car at the shop and a female friend of mine came along for the ride. The mechanic came out and she thought he was hot, so while I went inside to pay, she stayed out to flirt. When finally she got in my car, she looked disgusted. Seems when she went to hand him her number, she saw his hands, and he had dirt caked under his finger nails. I told her that's fairly normal for a grease monkey, but she said dirt under a guy's nails is an absolute deal breaker, no matter what his job description is. Why? Her answer sealed my grooming habits forever, and explained to me why some guys get regular manicures. She said that, when she's attracted to a guy, she immediately imagines having sex with him. And that starts with a lot of touching and caressing. But she finds the thought of a guy running his dirt encrusted nails all over her—and yes, inside her—completely disgusting. And he's toast.

She's not alone in her feeling this way either. A lot of women I know will look at a man's hands and sum up his entire grooming habits from them. For other women it's bad oral hygiene. Or if his clothes are neat and clean. Others judge by body odor, or if he's clean shaven. It depends on the woman, but your best bet is to pay attention to your grooming details.

WAR STORY: HER FINGERS SENT ME WALKING

Here's something that happened to me recently that backs up what I said about having good grooming habits and the importance of always making sure to take care of the little things:

I was in a mall last week, and saw a sign for a big sale at one of my favorite stores. I can always use a couple of new shirts, so I stopped in. I was looking at a display of solid color dress shirts, when I heard "Hi, can I help you?" I turned around to face this really adorable salesgirl wearing a sundress. Now, some guys love a chick in skintight jeans and some are turned on by woman in a business suit. Me? I have a weakness for sundresses. And this chick looked damn good in hers—she also had a beautiful smile and a fun personality to boot. Game on.

I did the usual when dealing with a woman who is paid to be nice and could possibly be earning commission on what you buy: I did the cocky and funny thing and made her my personal shopper. I dragged her all over the store, asked her to pick out what she thought would look best when I came to pick her up for our date. On and on down the golden path . . .

When I finally settled on what I wanted, I followed her to the register. She rang up my purchase, I slid my card through the reader, and she asked to see my ID. This is usually where I make some comment about her just wanting to have my address so she can stalk me, or that now I expect a birthday card since she knows my birthday. This in turn leads into how it's only fair if I get some of her personal info, her phone number for instance. But I didn't this time. Because when she reached for my driver's license, I noticed them. Her fingernails. They were disgusting. Not only had she chewed them all the way down, but it looked as though she had chewed the skin around them too. At that moment, it didn't matter that she was rocking the sundress or that her smile and personality were incredible. I was completely turned off.

I know it may sound shallow, but those chewed on fingers screamed that she was either extremely nervous, or incredibly anxiety-ridden. Maybe she had a lot of problems going on—or maybe was just plain dirty. And everything else went out the window in a split second. And if guys can flip the switch that fast—and we are a bunch of horndogs known for overlooking the biggest flaws for the sake of getting laid—imagine how easy it is for a woman to get turned off by something as small as dirt under your nails, or that clump of nose hairs peeking out from your nostril.

It's important to remember that you are constantly on the march when dating. So vary the places where you look to meet women depending on who you want to meet, and vary the kinds of dates you take them on. Remember that you'll want to eventually march her back to your place for a little horizontal marching. Keep your place, and yourself, in top shape, and she'll want to visit over and over again. But this still doesn't mean that there won't be some resistance or excuses. That goes with the territory, so you're going to have to learn how to handle it.

- Where you meet a girl says a lot about the type of girl she is. Bars and clubs are the most common places to meet women, but they are not necessarily the best places to do so. If you want to meet women, especially quality women, you need to go where they are, which means overcoming your Geographical Homophobia.
- By going to places, classes, and events that most guys consider "gay," you increase the girl-to-guy ratio exponentially, and increase your odds of meeting someone.
- Check the continuing education section of your local paper or Meetup.com for female-centric things to attend—and remember that dating does not always equal dinner or coffee. Think of something unique and exciting, so she thinks of you as more unique and exciting.
- Make sure your place is Date Worthy at all times. Use the Checklist of Things to Do Before She Comes Over to make sure.
- Have something you're really good at—a dish or a drink— that you can impress her with.
- Your grooming habits and how you live say a lot to her about you. Your looks? Not that important. Your grooming? Incredibly important.

CHAPTER 10

TERRAIN

"A foolish man tells a woman to stop talking, but a wise man tells her that her mouth is extremely beautiful when her lips are closed."

—Unknown

Sun Tzu knew that, even though he and his generals were highly trained and fully prepared, situations could arise that were ultimately out of his control. For instance the terrain he would be fighting on and which position his opponent decided to take, which would dictate the kind of resistance he would face during battle, weren't always details he could manage. While he couldn't physically change the ground the battle took place on, he could school himself in the dangers and unique characteristics of each different space and adjust his battle plans accordingly.

In dating, it isn't so much the actual terrain that can cause problems, but the metaphorical terrain of her position often presents resistance. While Sun Tzu encountered six types of terrain in battle, there are only three that relate to the type of resistance that you'll come up against—resistance that could find you at an impasse where she holds the advantage—unless you know what to do about it.

RESISTANCE: "LET'S JUST BE FRIENDS."

TERRAIN: ENTANGLING GROUND

Sun Tzu said that, "Ground that can be abandoned but is hard to reoccupy is called *Entangling*. If the enemy is prepared for you and you fail to defeat them, then, return being impossible, disaster will ensue."

SITUATION

How many times have you heard this: "I really like you, and you're a great guy, and any woman would be lucky to have you, but . . ." right before you find yourself relegated to the weird, sexless purgatory known as The Friend Zone? Most guys have heard it over and over. You find a great girl, you have a ton in common, you think things are progressing to the relationship stage (or at the very least, to the bedroom stage), and it turns out she doesn't think of you "in that way." If you abandon your position of wanting a sexual relationship, give in to her "friend request," and fail to defeat her resistance, you'll find that ground is nearly impossible to reoccupy.

WHY IT HAPPENED

Chances are you blew it during attraction building: 1) You either got too lazy and didn't start escalating the sexual tension, or 2) you did what Bobby did back in Chapter 6 and just hammered a conversation to death, putting yourself into the realm of "guy I just enjoy talking to." Or, maybe she simply wants to "out-value" you and take control by dictating the terms of your relationship, until *she* decides to let it progress further. Either way, her Attraction Engine has stalled out and you have to get it fired back up.

RESULT IF YOU DON'T TAKE ACTION

If you don't get her fired back up, you'll end up as just another one of her girlfriends. You'll get to be the one she calls to complain about the guys who are drilling her like she was the last remaining off-shore oil deposit. And if you want to spend time with her, you get to take her shopping and hold her purse while she tries on lingerie she'll wear to please that asshat she's dating who treats her like a disposable sex toy. All while following her around like a lost puppy waiting for her to realize you're the one for her and finally throw you a bone. Sound like the situation a High-Value Alpha Male would be in? Yeah, not so much.

BATTLE PLAN

First you need to make a decision—is this girl worth fighting for? If not, you can tell her you're not interested in being friends. You have enough friends, and your busy social calendar doesn't have room to squeeze in a woman who isn't interested in a physical relationship. Period.

Here, you position yourself as a man who doesn't give in to a woman's desires, doesn't let her call the shots, and doesn't hang around until she exhausts all other options and finally decides to give you a shot—if that ever happens. Your goal is to meet a woman who wants to move into a relationship. Or, hell, even just the bedroom. If that's not the case, then you're walking. And be prepared to walk, which shouldn't be a hard decision because, in all honesty, do you really want to just "hang out" and be her personal ego booster if you are attracted to her and she doesn't feel the same way? Of course not. So walking shouldn't be any sweat off your stones.

And here's the upside: When a woman knows you don't have a problem bailing, she'll usually start to reconsider her decision. Again, it comes down to value. By telling her "No thanks. You're a great girl, but I have enough friends, so take care," you display a higher value by not letting her dictate how your relationship is going to be, calling her out on the fact that she doesn't have the balls to blow you off entirely, and then taking matters into your own hands. This can get her Attraction Engine started up again.

COUNTER ATTACKS

But what if she's starting to lean toward just being friends and you want to pull her back from the edge? There are a couple of things you can do. First, you can try the same "I'm going to walk" routine, but this time with a slight twist: Hit her with your direct intention as you end it. Something like, "I appreciate you want to be friends, but in all honesty I'm very attracted to you—you're a smart, funny, attractive, and very sexy woman—so I don't see you as just a friend. And I'm not going to apologize for feeling that way. So if you want to add me to your list of girlfriends, or be able to call me only when you need something heavy moved, I'm not interested." Sometimes this can be enough to jar her into thinking of you in a sexual way, if she wasn't thinking of you like that before.

Another way to ward off being relegated to The Friend Zone, is to give her exactly what she wants: Treat her as a friend. Just like you would any of the guys. And that means not kissing her ass, or jumping just because she said jump. Because if one of your guy friends called early on a Saturday morning and said he needed a ride to the mall, you'd tell him to go fuck himself and hang up. She gets the same treatment. After all, she's a friend.

Treating her like a friend also means telling her she needs to fix you up with her hot horny friends. Especially the redhead. Or at the very least come out for drinks and help you meet women. And if she refuses? Then call her on her shit, like you would any of your friends. "You didn't want to have a sexual relationship with me. Now you won't help me meet someone who does. Why did you want to be friends with me in the first place? Was it so I could just do stuff for you?" And one of two things will happen: she'll either realize she just wanted someone to prop up her ego and be her Moodle, or she'll snap out of her haze, see you as the High-Value Alpha Male you are, realize she didn't want to fix you up with anyone else because it made her jealous, and see that she really is attracted to you. Either way, you win.

RESISTANCE: "I HAVE A BOYFRIEND"

TERRAIN: NARROW PASS

"With regard to *Narrow Passes*," advices Sun Tzu, "should the enemy forestall you in occupying a pass, do not go after them if the pass if fully garrisoned, but only if it is weakly garrisoned."

SITUATION

You've met a great girl. There's definitely some mutual attraction, the sexual tension is building, and then she slams everything to a halt by saying she has a boyfriend. Note: I'm assuming she brought it up, and you didn't do something boneheaded like *ask* her if she had a boyfriend. You never, ever ask that question. Why? Because 1) You always assume she does, since she's hot and desirable, and 2) When you bring it up, you instantly toss a grenade into any attraction you've built.

WHY IT HAPPENED

Because it always happens. The fact is most hot, desirable women have boyfriends. They tell you because they either want you to know so you don't think this is going any further (a fully garrisoned pass), or they need to remind themselves because they are starting to feel attracted to you and they need the reinforcement (a weakly garrisoned pass). Lucky for you, most of the time it's the second one.

RESULT IF YOU DON'T TAKE ACTION

You miss out on a chance at a great girl. If every guy who was told this decided to say, "I'm sorry, I had no idea. Enjoy the rest of your evening," and walked away, no one would get laid. Note: This is only in the case of boyfriends. Not husbands. There is a special place in Hell for guys who continue to move forward when they find out she is married.

BATTLE PLAN

Understand something: I'm not advocating being a home wrecker (see note above), or that you try to pry a girl away from another guy. But the fact is there are a lot of women out there in unhappy relationships. (If you have female friends who call you when things aren't going well, you know what I'm talking about.) *And the stability of their relationship is not your concern.* It's hers. For better or for worse, there are a lot of people who won't leave one relationship, no matter how shitty, until they find another. So I salute your moral nobility if you want to wait for girls to be completely single before you approach them, but I promise you that you'll be waiting a long, long time. The best women are *never* single. She'll stand by their man faithfully forever—until something better comes along and shows her what she's been missing. That something is you.

You have no idea how stable the relationship is, or why she's even still in it. Maybe she's just with him so she won't be alone. Maybe she's locked in "golden handcuffs" and needs his financial support. Or maybe she's lying through her teeth and there is no other guy. It doesn't matter. Her relationship status is *her* concern. Unless you want to disqualify 85 to 90 percent of the women you meet, you have to learn to take it with a grain of salt if she says she has a man.

And when she does say she has a boyfriend, read her body language and pay attention to how she says it. For example, if she's still facing you, looking in your eyes, and says something that almost sounds like a question: "Well, you know I have a boyfriend . . . " or "That sounds wonderful, too bad I'm seeing someone . . . " chances are very good she's looking for you to keep going and give her an excuse to ditch him. She has weakly garrisoned the pass. If she turns from you and very assertively says, "I appreciate the attention, but I'm in a wonderful relationship, so have a good night," you might as well move on. She has that pass strongly garrisoned; I'm not saying it would be impossible to change her mind, but it would be a long and uphill battle where the rewards don't outweigh the risks.

COUNTER ATTACKS

If she's giving off signals that say she's attracted to you, just treat her boyfriend announcement like a minor annoyance and simply plow on. You know from your own intel that her telling you she has a boyfriend is solely for her benefit, not yours. She's trying to reconcile in her head that she's got someone, even though she is very attracted to you. So she serves up a weak defense in the subconscious hope that you'll crash through it. (At least that's the mindset you have to have.) So ignore it, tease her about it, pretend to be momentarily horrified, role play how you'll help her plan her escape, do anything but show any signs that it matters to you that there is someone else. Why? Because you know that you're the better option and that she's foolish if she doesn't see it.

Most guys assume that it's a polite blow off or the end of the line when a woman says she has a boyfriend. Not so. It could be just another Shit Test where she's drawing you into that pass to see if you decide to keep fighting, or to turn tail and run. You, recognizing her very weakly garrisoned pass, know better and keep advancing. So when you invite her for coffee and she plays the boyfriend card counter with, "Well he's not invited. I'm only inviting you. So 4:30 it is then. Table for two."

You can also fire back your own Shit Test, and engage her jealousy buttons, by responding, "Well I have a girlfriend, so it shouldn't be a problem. I'll see you at 9." If she starts asking about your girlfriend, make her as ridiculously over the top as possible. "Well, she is a lingerie model, so she's out of town a lot shooting at exotic locations. This weekend she's in Barbados, so she won't catch us . . . ." Even though she knows you're playing with her, it still pushes her competitive buttons.

A more sinister approach is to attack the poor bastard himself. It's bad enough he's not there to defend himself and his girlfriend is caught in your web—now you're going to start chipping away at his character and their relationship in her mind. How? By referring to him as her "Borefriend." By pointing out that she is out for a fun night out, and where is he? Doesn't he want to enjoy time with her? By suggesting that he is probably out with his buddies right now having a few beers and hitting on girls. The list of Boyfriend Busters is endless.

Stoking her desire for fantasy and mystery always works when you role play with a girl. Start plotting how you're going to "rescue" her from this guy: "Okay, so here's what we'll do. We'll wait until after sundown. That way he won't see my car. You tell him you're going out with the girls, and hide a change of clothes in the bushes. Right at 8:14, I'll drive around the corner and you dash out the front door . . . ." If you handle it right, she'll get so caught up in playing along, she'll forget what's-his-name.

RESISTANCE: "UM, I REALLY SHOULDN'T BE DOING THIS"

TERRAIN: PRECIPITOUS HEIGHTS

Sun Tzu sees Precipitous Heights as the higher ground taken by the opponent. And he advises you "precede your adversary, occupy the raised and sunny spots, and wait there for them to come up." In our case, we aren't going to occupy the physical high ground, but the moral high ground.

SITUATION

A lot of times your target will already be occupying the moral higher ground, and will put up some "Last Minute Resistance," deciding she shouldn't be doing the naughty things you're doing— regardless of how much she's enjoying it or how badly she wants you.

WHY IT HAPPENED

Because she's been told her entire life that "Good Girls" just don't do these things with guys they've just met. Only "sluts" do. This is why Last Minute Resistance is also commonly known as the Good Girl Defense or Anti-Slut Defense. Her body wants to keep going, but her brain is telling her this is bad behavior. And she doesn't want you judging her—even though her skirt is already hiked up over her head and you're wearing her panties as a face mask.

BATTLE PLAN

First you need to establish if this is a serious "No, stop right now" situation, or just her dealing with the conflicting thoughts in her head. Her tone and body language will tell you, and if you see it's a definite, "No!" it's game over and you stop. Period. If it's a case of her looking to you make her feel comfortable with what she's doing, then you need to do exactly that. As Sun Tzu says, "If the enemy has occupied Precipitous Heights, do not follow them, but retreat and try to entice them away."

COUNTER ATTACKS

Take Sun Tzu's advice and retreat. Then try to entice her away. So when she says, "Stop, I shouldn't be doing this" the first thing you do is stop. Immediately. Because by continuing on you start to cross the line from "Guy I'm Really Attracted To" to "Handsy Creep Who Won't Stop When Told." And there's no coming back from that. (Not that I blame her.) The key to dealing with her Anti-Slut Defense is comfort. She needs to feel comfortable that she is not a bad girl, that you are not judging her, and that you don't see her as just a sex toy. Keep up with the groping and egging her on and you reinforce all those negatives, which only serves to cement her position on that high ground.

So how do you make her feel comfortable? By agreeing with her. When you hit her with the typical douchebag response of, "Come on baby, you know you want this as much as I do . . ." all you're doing is reinforcing that she wants to do something she sees, right or wrong, as "bad." But when you take the stigma away by saying something like, "I know, this is crazy. I just got carried away . . . we need to slow down . . ." you do three things: 1) You take the "bad behavior" off of her, 2) You give her an "out" by blaming it on you being so attracted to her you got "carried away," other than her being a slut, and 3) You show her that you are okay with stopping and that this isn't just a "conquest at all costs" for you.

Giving her something else to blame the behavior on is key. We all know that women love sex just as much, if not more, than we do. It's just not proper for them to brag about it. Have you ever noticed when you're talking to a female friend and she's telling a story about something really naughty or slutty or "bad girl" that she did, there's always an excuse tied to it? "So, I grabbed the waiter's crotch and told him, I've got a tip for ya! But it's okay, it was Kathy's bachelorette party, and we were all drunk on watermelontinis . . ." or ". . . and I took him back to my hotel room and told him I'd show him a real 'marketing initiative' . . . I know, but it was a business trip and you know what happens during those things . . . ." Women need excuses to take the guilt off of their sexuality. Give them to her and take the blame.

Once she gets comfortable again, you can start ramping the heat back up. Odds are that she'll let you go a little further than last time. And if she starts to resist again, retreat and try to entice her away again. Every time you gain ground, you may end up hitting on one of her resistance points. Every woman has different areas of sex that she feels she needs to resist. Once you encounter one of hers, it'll trigger her response and you'll have to stop until she gets comfortable and let's you advance; it's sort of a "two steps forward, one step back" dance.

WAR STORY: SHE DUMPED THE GROOM, AND MARRIED THE VIDEOGRAPHER

You'd think a little something like an upcoming marriage would make the terrain seriously uncrossable—especially if you're hired to work the wedding.

I have a friend I'll call Caroline to protect her identity, even though this is her favorite story to tell and everyone who knows her has already heard it. Three months before Caroline was to walk down the aisle, she was interviewing videographers to capture the ceremony for posterity. Kristoff (not his real name either) was one of the camera jockeys she went to meet.

After he showed her some samples and they got ready to talk costs, he told her he wasn't going to quote her a price because he wasn't going to let her get married. At least not to whoever the guy was she was planning on marrying. His reason? The guy she was really meant to marry was him. And, should she decide to ignore him and go through with the wedding anyway, he jokingly said he might even show up at the church and tell the priest he objects.

Gotta give him credit for a ballsy move. You'd think that having a woman you've just met say that she is getting married in a few short weeks would deter a guy from telling her she was really meant to be with him. Apparently not.

Even though Caroline left and said it would never happen, Kristoff kept at it. Not, she says, in a creepy stalker sort of way, but in cocky and funny sort of way. Of course she was flattered, and they became friends. So when she found out a couple of weeks later that her fiancé had some skeletons in his closet that were big enough and scary enough to leave her without any doubts that she needed to call off the wedding, friend Kristoff was there for her. Like he's been every day since they got married to each other seventeen years—and three kids—ago.

Does this mean I want you to scour the engagement announcements in your local paper trolling for prospective targets? That's not an entirely bad idea, but no, of course not. What it proves is that when Kristoff met the girl he knew in his heart he wanted to spend the rest of his life with, it didn't matter that she was about to marry someone else. He dealt with the terrain he was on, and crossed it.

There's a strong chance you're going to encounter some kind of resistance during any mission—in fact, it would be strange if everything went smoothly. But when it's expected and you're prepared, the chances of that resistance torpedoing you are minimal. Unfortunately, these three types of terrain aren't all you're going to have to go up against. You also have to watch out for what Sun Tzu calls "The Nine Situations." And you'll discover what they are in the next chapter.

- There are three types of terrain you need to watch out for, each of which can cause resistance to the completion of your mission.
- The first is the Let's Just Be Friends resistance. She may not be attracted to you, or maybe she's just being polite and doesn't want to blow you off. Either way, the Friend Zone is not a place you want to be. If you're here, either tell her straight up you'd rather not be "just friends" and end it, or treat her like you would any of your other friends.
- The second type of resistance is the I Have a Boyfriend defense. Understand that the vast majority of women already have boyfriends. And the reasons she's not leaving him are many.
- If you don't at least press forward a little, depending on how she told you, you could miss out on a great girl. After all, the stability of her relationship, and why she's out drinking and talking to strange men without her boyfriend, is not your concern. It's hers.
- This rule only applies for boyfriends, not husbands. Women with husbands are off limits.
- The third type of resistance is the Last Minute Resistance, also known as the Good Girl Defense or the Anti-Slut Defense. She is either doing this to convince you that she is not a bad girl, or to convince herself of that same fact.
- Read her body language and voice. There's a big difference between a firm, definite "No!" and a somewhat

conflicted "I really don't think I should be doing this." A definite "No" means you stop immediately.

- To counter attack Last Minute Resistance, use Sun Tzu's advice of retreating and trying to entice them away. It becomes a "two steps forward, one step back" dance.

CHAPTER 11

THE NINE SITUATIONS

"When women go wrong, men go right after them."
—Mae West

In warfare, Sun Tzu noticed nine specific situations that his generals needed to be aware of, look out for, and leverage for victory. Not wanting his men caught with their pants down in battle should any of these situations arise, he gave them specific tactics for dealing with each.

Sun Tzu said, "The skillful tactician may be likened to the *shuai-jan*. Now the *shuai-jan* is a snake found in the Ch'ang mountains. Strike at its head and you will be attacked by the tail; strike at its tail, and you will be attacked by its head; strike at its middle, and you will be attacked by head and tail both." You have to be the same way when you are out in the field. No matter what happens or what part of you is attacked, you have to use everything in your arsenal to ensure victory. There are a lot of snafus that can happen when you're out there in the heat of battle, so you have to keep your wits about you and know which of the situations to look for—and which to look out for.

SITUATION 1: IS SHE INTERESTED?

So how do you tell if a woman is really digging you when the Bitch Shields are up and the bullshit is flying? Look for specific physical and verbal indicators that'll clue you in, even as she's trying hard to play hard to get.

PHYSICAL INDICATORS OF INTEREST

Kino: Originally coined by Ross Jeffries, the founder of Speed Seduction and considered "the father of modern seduction" by Neil Strauss, kino is any kind of touching that involves you both—either she touches you or allows you to touch her. This includes her touching your arm, brushing your leg, and giving you a playful punch when you say something funny directed at her. It also includes letting you put your hand on her back or hip, hold her hand, or kiss her on the cheek.

Eye Contact: If she lingers a little longer than usual when looking into your eyes—or, even better, stares longingly into your eyes—you're in.

Primping: If she starts to absentmindedly fix her hair or straighten her dress, she's subconsciously telling you she wants to look good for you.

Body Language: If she moves closer to you, leans in to hear you better, or doesn't reflexively pull back her hand or arm when you reach for it, she's feeling more comfortable with you and the attraction is escalating. Also, look for her to bite or wet her lips or fidget with her jewelry or drink; these are all telltale signs she's getting attracted.

VERBAL INDICATORS OF INTEREST

Laughter: Women are a comic's toughest audience. If she laughs at your jokes or stories, she digs you—especially if she calls bullshit on you, while still laughing.

Compliments: Women rarely compliment anyone unless they like them or are comfortable around them. If she points out something about your personality or something you're wearing, you've chipped away at her defenses.

Conversation: If you're not the only one talking and she's constantly coming back at you, even if it's to disagree or be completely sarcastic, she's interested. Otherwise you'd be hearing a whole lot of "uh huhs" and "yeahs."

Shit Tests: As we've seen over and over, Shit Tests are her all-purpose weapon of choice. If you've been talking to her for a while, and the Shit Tests are still coming, she's still qualifying you. If she wasn't interested, she would have stopped way before now.

SITUATION 2: GRENADES, COCKBLOCKERS, AND OTHER OBSTACLES

Often when you're out on a mission, the chick you're targeting isn't the problem. Instead, there are a variety of bogies coming in from all angles, all intent, consciously or subconsciously, on blowing it for you. Here's how to handle them.

GRENADES

A grenade is one of your target's friends who is either miserable with her own life, or a self-appointed Mother Hen hell bent on keeping her flock intact. A grenade will do whatever it takes to torpedo your game. It's your wingman's job to occupy her, but what happens if you're flying solo?

First you need to pay attention to the grenade. Usually this is enough to disarm her, especially if part of why she's giving you a hard time is because she's craving attention. But if she's not settling down and continues to try to dive bomb you, you're going to have to fight fire with fire; and that means coming back at her with what she's giving. If she's trying to drag her friend away from you, ask her if she's her court appointed guardian. If she's interrupting you while you're talking to your target, call her on it and tell her it's rude to interrupt.

You can involve your target too. Ask her if her friend is always this much of a bitch or drama queen and why she hangs out with her. In my personal experience, if the chick is into you, she'll usually tell her friend to back off.

COCKBLOCKERS, DRUNKS, AND JEALOUS ALPHA MALES

These obstacles are unavoidable in most group situations, like in a bar or club, and they don't have to come from a stranger or a rival. One of your buddies is just as likely to step in your way as a stranger is—especially when you mix alcohol with a hot babe and add a dash of jealousy. Your best move is to isolate the girl from the situation, take her outside or move to another table. If this doesn't work, you're going to have to engage.

Now I don't mean that you should drop gloves and start swinging. That may have worked in high school, but back then the biggest consequence was going to the principal's office or getting your ass kicked. As an adult, those consequences are much stiffer, and can include jail time and lawsuits. So use your words, not your hands.

Your first tactic is to befriend your obstacle and bore the shit out of him. Ask him where he's from. Where he got that shirt. If he hangs out here a lot. Where he works . . . all the fluff talk that people hate. It'll usually have a calming effect on him and he'll settle down. Then you can start hitting him with subtle insults disguised as compliments, and make him look foolish in front of the girl. "Hey man, where did you get that shirt? It's awesome! I didn't know you could get those anymore. Love it. I want you as my personal style guru." She'll get it. He likely won't. And if he does get it and you think he's going to escalate the situation? Just tell him you were just busting balls, because that's what friends do. And you're friends now, right? He'll feel like an asshole.

BORING BUDDY

Anyone can have a bad night. But some guys have a bad career when it comes to meeting women. And there are times when the guy you're hanging out with falls into the latter category. If you're hanging with a friend who isn't holding up his end of the conversation when you're talking to a group of women, you run the risk of losing them to boredom. More so if he's telling really bad jokes, bringing up negative topics, or is just standing there with a blank look.

The best way to handle this is to go into a set alone. If he trails over, then it's your job as a friend and wingman to throw him a lifeline. Talk him up. Bring up funny stories that involve him so he's included even if he doesn't speak. That way he's not an anchor around your neck.

SITUATION 3: IT GOES NEGATIVE

Your goal is to turn the conversation sexy at your first chance and up the attraction level, so stay away from negative topics and don't get dragged into a conversation that is turning negative. You want her to associate you with fun and humor and excitement—which isn't going to happen if you're talking about how crappy the economy is, how you lost your job, or how two of your buddies have to declare bankruptcy. You may think she'll keep talking to you if those topics are brought up, but it's a dangerous road to go down—one that rarely ends in her bedroom.

Other topics to avoid include politics, religion, past relationships, health problems, money problems, family problems, her problems (you want to date her, not analyze her), how much you hate crowds, how shitty the music is, or anything else that is negative or argumentative. If things start to turn in this direction, it's your job to guide them to a more positive place. For example, if she starts complaining about how crowded it is, tell her that you'd probably never have met if it wasn't so full of people and a popular place to be.

SITUATION 4: REWARDING BAD BEHAVIOR

Want to know the secret of why some women are so bitchy and awful to men? Simple. They've been rewarded for that behavior—and we are to blame. This is another one of the toughest things for most guys to get through their heads and it goes back to us wanting to be "nice" to women. Like Pavlov's dogs, we've trained them to think that when they bitch at us, threaten us, or treat us badly, we get overly nice so they don't leave us. Sounds really embarrassing when it's laid out like that, doesn't it?

So, when a woman is shitty to you, or is demanding, whiny, pissy, or in any way just plain bad, the best plan is to do the opposite of what she says. For example, if she demands—in a nasty way—that you call her more, start calling even less. It'll reinforce that when she's a bitch, you'll respond accordingly. You want her to ask nicely, and you can reward her when she does, but not before.

SITUATION 5: MATERIAL GIRLS

She wants you to buy her drinks, dinner, or gifts, and so you comply to show her how much you like her and are willing to do for her. You think you're in, but you're actually dead wrong. All you've done is lower your value and give in to her demands, which actually makes her lose respect for you. Ever have a conversation with a stripper? They picture all men as walking wallets—only with less intelligence. They are masters at wringing buckets of money from lonely suckers who think the path to their bedroom is lined with twenties. You, on the other hand, know to only buy a woman something when she earns it.

SITUATION 6: "I KNOW WHAT YOU'RE DOING . . . "

Every once in a while you're going to run into a chick who knows "The Game" and will call you out on it. She may be the target or you may be going after one of her friends but, whoever she is, she revels in being "smart" enough and savvy enough to recognize your shenanigans. Your best defense is to deflect the "pick up" label she's going to put on what you're up to. Instead, tell her all you're doing is trying to meet her or attempting to see if she's worthy of trying to meet. This displays higher value and puts it on her to prove she is worthy.

If (actually when) she asks you how many women you've tried this on (because they *all* do), play it up. Tell her it's "thousands," and you spend hours each night just throwing out lines and gaming women. Then, since she knows so much about it, ask her if she wants to be your wingwoman so you can pick up women together. Don't shy away from it. Instead, own it and play with her. Just because she knows what you're up to doesn't mean she doesn't want to play.

SITUATION 7: DEFLECTING HIGH-POWERED BITCH SHIELDS

There are Bitch Shields, and then there are BITCH SHIELDS. Occasionally you'll run into a chick brandishing one with the intention of smashing it over your head. It could be that she's bitter from a past relationship or maybe she's so tired of getting hit on that her defensive walls have gotten more and more prickly. But turning tail and running is not an option. Even if you don't want her, there's a chance that you may later target one of her friends, or at least a chick nearby, and you don't want her to come in and torpedo your chances. Your best option is to hit her with a compliment that contains a thinly veiled insult. Something that shows you're not impressed or intimidated by her, such as, "I like your hair. Extensions?" or "I love that dress you have on. There was a chick here a minute ago wearing the same one. Now *she* looked great in it."

SITUATION 8: SHOOTING DOWN HER OBJECTIONS

Just like with Bitch Shields and chicks who "know what you're up to," when you run into any objections as to why a woman can't date you, you should never turn defensive and try to prove yourself worthy. By now you should realize that this only lowers your value in her eyes. Instead, go right at it. Have a comeback ready that shows she's crazy for thinking you're too old, too young, too skinny, too much of a player, or too whatever for her. Because you're not "too old"; unlike the little boys she dates, you're "a man who is experienced and knows what he's doing." You're not "too young"; you're "willing and eager to learn, and want a sexy older woman to guide you."

SITUATION 9: CONFRONTED BY "THE PROTECTOR"

Have you ever watched one of those nature shows where two alpha males get together in the wild? There's always a confrontation that ultimately decides who gets to rule the herd. Well, the same thing happens when two Alpha Males get together in a bar—especially if one of them feels you're trying to mow his lawn.

Unlike the typical drunk cockblocker or jealous Alpha you encountered in Situation 2, this guy feels it's his duty to protect the women in his group from guys like you, and he's willing to do it forcefully and physically. Your clever comments laced with sarcasm meant to cut him down and embarrass him will only make him angrier—and leave him wanting to smack the smartass right out of you. But you also don't want to look like a pussy and hurt your chances with any of the other women in the place, so apologizing for nothing (hitting on women in a bar is not only perfectly okay, it's the reason nature created bars in the first place) is also a bad idea. Normally, it's your wingman's job to keep the Protector busy long enough for you to close the deal, get her number, and get out in one piece. But if you don't have an experienced wingman who will talk this guy down, you're going to have to diffuse this human bomb yourself.

Start by questioning his intention: "Hey, we're all just here having a good time. I'm not fucking with you or anyone else. Look, everyone else was smiling and laughing . . . why are *you* so upset?" Usually this will make him realize he's being unreasonable in his reaction to you, but not always. And that's when you need to breakout the old faithful that got you through all those days of elementary school recess when the bullies would circle: you befriend him. Not in a roll over and show your belly way, but game him like you would any of the women. Show him you're willing to let this go and have a good time, but as an equal and not as one of his hangers on. Say something like, "Hey, I see you're an Alpha. I am too. A lot of chumps in this place have just let me run all over them, but not you. I can respect that." Once he sees that you're a guy just out to have some fun and not encroach on his "herd," he'll usually calm down.

WAR STORY: COCKBLOCKING PROTECTOR TORPEDOES HIMSELF

Sometimes the more defenses that are up and the more focused someone is that you are not getting near a girl, the easier it is to score . . .

A while back, when I had just moved to South Florida and didn't know anyone in town, a guy I met at work invited me over to his place for a party he was throwing for his wife. I was single at the time, but he told me there wouldn't be any single women there because their friends were all couples. This didn't matter to me because, after a couple of weeks of hanging around my studio apartment, watching TV, and working on school projects, I needed a night out—regardless of whether I'd have a shot at taking home a hottie or not.

I got to the party, introductions were made, and the requisite small talk ensued. But there was one couple that kept pretty much to themselves. She was a hot Latina who was trying hard to not make too much eye contact with anyone. He was an overpumped meathead who spent his time glaring around the room, almost daring anyone to venture close. I asked my buddy what the story was, and it turns out the chick was a college classmate of his wife's, and Meathead was her boyfriend of about three or four months. The reason for the don't-fuck-with-me demeanor? Apparently there was another guy at the party who had dated Hot

Latina before they got together, and Meathead was gonna make sure that there was no chance an old flame might get rekindled. So he stood guard and she was not allowed out of his sight.

Cut to a couple of hours—and a whole lot of drinks—later. I'm talking to a couple in the living room about my decision to go back to school and get my second degree in design rather than go to law school, and I hear yelling coming from the kitchen. Not the "Oh shit, I burned the roast" yelling, but the "I'm going to fucking kill you" kind of yelling. My buddy's wife comes running out scared to death and looking for help.

I run into the kitchen and see Meathead and Mr. Ex squaring off around the center island. Turns out Mr. Ex said something to Hot Latina that really set Meathead off—something really inappropriate like "Hey, how have you been?"—and now Meathead wants to make sure Mr. Ex's jaw is wired shut so he won't be able to talk to her ever again. Hot Latina is near tears and begging them to stop. My buddy is trying to talk sense into Meathead, but you know how effective that can be when a guy like that has an overload of testosterone mixed with alcohol pumping through his system. The whole situation is one big powder keg that's about to blow up—taking my buddy and his kitchen with it. Naturally, not wanting to lose my only friend in Miami to Death by 'Roid Raging Maniac, I stepped into the middle of it.

First I told my buddy to escort Mr. Ex out of the party and send him home. Having the catalyst for another potential explosion around was not a good idea. Then I turned to Meathead and tried to reason with him. I told him I wasn't taking sides, wasn't there to trade blows with anyone, and that I completely understood why he was pissed off. Then I told him that, since the guy was gone, there was no more threat to his relationship with his girl. And besides, this was neither the time nor the place to settle this anyway. My buddy and his wife were just trying to have a nice dinner party, and to ruin the whole evening and trash their place over something so stupid was not fair to them. I asked him calmly to please apologize to our hosts and other guests, and then leave. With nothing left to posture over, he agreed.

As they went to leave, Hot Latina said a quick thank you for helping to end the situation without the need for police and ambulances. "Sure, no problem," I said. "You just make sure you get home safely."

Once they were gone, my buddy's wife came over to me and told me Hot Latina had asked her to give me her number—and that she wanted me to call her the next day so she could thank me properly. So I did. And she did. She told me that she had ended it with Meathead that night. She couldn't see herself dating a guy like that. So, what kind of guy could she see herself dating? The guy she ended up dating for the next three years. Me.

So let's take a look at what happened. I wasn't trying to pick up Hot Latina, but there ended up being a strong attraction; one that ignited quickly, even with her defensive shields up and a Protector by her side. How? Because two things happened once the fight started and I stepped in: 1) She saw him for the over-jealous jackass he was, and 2) my actions set off all three of her Attraction Fuel bells: I showed Strength of Character for stepping in and trying to put an end to what was about to become a bad situation even though I didn't have to. I demonstrated both Fearlessness, by getting in between two guys who were jacked up and ready to throw down, and Loyalty, to my friend who was about to have his house turned upside down for no good reason. And it didn't hurt that she was now disgusted by Meathead for the way he handled himself and saw his true nature. All of which added up to me scoring a prime pick up, without actually picking up.

When you're meeting women you want to be sharp, alert, and on your toes. Things happen fast and situations can change in an instant. It's one of the reasons why I advise you save your heavy drinking for nights out with the boys and keep the consumption light when you roll out for women. You need a clear head to deal with whatever they throw at you—and to be able to use some of the advanced tips, tricks, and tactics that you'll learn about in the next chapter.

POST-TRAINING DEBRIEFING

- There are exactly nine situations you need to be on the lookout for when out on a mission. The Nine Situations are:

1. Is She Interested?: She's going to be hiding behind her Bitch Shield and flinging a ton of bullshit. You need to look for her specific physical and verbal indicators that will tell you that she's digging you, even if her mouth isn't. Look for kino, eye contact, primping, body language on the physical side, and laughter, compliments and conversation on the verbal side. Even the continuation of Shit Tests can tell you that you still have a shot.

2. Grenades, Cockblockers, and Other Obstacles: Your target isn't the only one who can blow holes in an otherwise solid mission. There are a variety of bogeys that can come at you from all angles, with the sole intention of torpedoing your game.

3. It Goes Negative: You want to be fun and exciting, right? Then stay away from topics that turn your conversation negative like politics, the economy, health problems, money issues, even how crowded the bar is.

4. Rewarding Bad Behavior: If you treat her nice when she's being nasty, you're not showing her what a willing and supportive guy you are. Instead, all you're doing is letting he know that it's okay to shit on you.

5. Material Girls: Constantly buying her things like drinks, gifts, and dinners, especially early in the relationship, will make you look like a walking wallet.

6. "I Know What You're Doing": She's read "The Game" and watched *The Pickup Artist*, and she revels in being wise to your shenanigans. Own up to it and play with her. Just because she knows what you're up to doesn't mean she doesn't want to play.

7. Deflecting High-Powered Bitch Shields: Some women have taken their Bitch Shields way past Threat Level Orange. You've got to tread lightly and eject carefully, so you don't blow your chances with her friends or nearby targets.

8. Shooting Down Her Objections: When she gives you reasons why she can't date you, don't get all defensive. Go right back at it and have a comeback that proves she's crazy for thinking that way.

9. Confronted by "The Protector": He feels it's his duty to protect the women of the group from guys like you. By any means necessary. If you're flying solo and don't have a wingman to keep him busy, you're going to have to talk him down yourself. Questioning his intentions and showing him how he's overreacting to a harmless situation should do the trick.

- Know how to handle each of those, and you're chances of being snagged in a trap go way down.
- You need to be prepared for whatever is thrown your way. So keep your head clear and your wits about you. This is why drunken pickups rarely work out.

CHAPTER 12

ATTACK BY FIRE

"Love is the only dirty trick played on us to achieve continuation of the species."

—William Somerset Maugham

In Sun Tzu's day, battles weren't always fought solely with swords from horseback, or with archers launching arrows from afar. Sometimes, the situation called for something a little more bad ass—and that's when Sun Tzu would break out the equivalent of today's anti-tank missile: Fire.

Sun Tzu warns, "In order to carry out an attack with fire, we must have means available; the material for raising fire should always be kept in readiness." Whether used to burn an enemy's camp, supplies, or munitions, or hurled at them with catapults and flaming arrows to create fear and confusion and overwhelm the enemy, fire was his version of shock and awe. Not to be used every time, but sparingly when the situation called for it.

Consider the following tips, tricks, and tactics as your fire. Essential in winning the battle, they are not to be overused and spread around like breadcrumbs in front of pigeons, but rather treated with respect for the power they hold in helping you achieve your goals. Some are clever. Some are just plain common sense, taken to a new level. And some are seriously insidious. Some may even seem corny and stupid, but all are highly effective, and will help you take your battlefield skills to the next level. You have absolutely nothing to lose (except maybe your loneliness in bed). Keep in mind that I'm not presenting an exhaustive list here—because what you can use is almost endless. This is just to get you started.

Also, keep in mind that all of these have been field-tested and used successfully—and I didn't come up with any of them. They all come from the websites and reports of both well-known pioneers in the art of seduction, and regular guys who are working hard to increase their success with women. I've added an attribution where one was available. Most (along with hundreds of others) can be found on FastSeduction.com (*www.fastseduction*.com), a tremendous resource for continuing your education.

Disclaimer: Some of this is real Evil Genius shit. And I can't be held responsible for you actually putting it to use, nor the consequences of your actions.

GIMMICKS

Palm reading. Astrology. Handwriting analysis. Psychic readings. "Best Friends" tests. These are all things that guys consider pure and utter nonsense. But to women this stuff is chick crack. It plays directly into their sense of fantasy and mystery, and they can't get enough of it. So not only does pulling one of these out of your bag of tricks propel you way past every other guy she's talked to tonight, it'll also get her begging you for more. As a bonus, *you* become the person she associates with that fantasy and mystery. And, as an added bonus, using one of the gimmicks like palm reading allows you to build even more attraction by making things physical when you hold her hand.

Do you need to be a palm reading expert or a real psychic to pull it off? Of course not. Are any of those charlatans who charge real money for these things actual experts or psychics? Please. It's more about the fun and excitement of it than it is about being accurate. But if you are going to read her palm or analyze her handwriting, I highly recommend reading up on the basics so you know which is her love line, life line, fate line, etc., and don't end up blowing it by getting one of the foundations wrong.

Whatever technique you use, and I go over them in the next few pages, just be sure that everything you say is positive and makes her feel special. You are also going to use it to amp up the sexual tension.

COLD READING

First, you need to be comfortable when performing a cold reading. This is a technique "psychics" use to "read" you and your future. And all it consists of is spewing out general information anyone who is paying close attention could see, along with some stuff most women desperately want associated with themselves— like love and passion and inner secrets she longs for someone to know about—then applying it to one of the gimmicks here. Play it off like you are looking deep into her soul, and her Bitch Shield will drop faster than home values in Vegas. And pointing out that she's not what she appears to be on the surface is pure gold. For example: "I get that you are a person who relates to her friends, but has a much deeper side she wishes they could see." Or, "You look like this sweet, innocent girl, but I get the feeling that there is a naughty side no one knows about . . . ."

PALM READING

Focus on her love line when you apply cold reading to palm reading. Make sure you don't rely solely on her love line, or she'll see it as a game. For example, bring up how her life line shows a real love for life, and how her brain line shows underlying intelligence, but with emotions in conflict, and the need to express them creatively.

HANDWRITING ANALYSIS

For handwriting analysis, have her write something on a piece of paper or cocktail napkin; like her name, email address and phone number for instance. Show her how the loops and angles of her letters reveal the secrets she's been keeping, the deeper qualities of her personality that no other guys have picked up on. She'll eat it up.

BEST FRIENDS TESTS

Women love to take tests. It's been the bread and butter of women's magazines for decades. So with quick tests, like the "Best Friends Test" (first developed by Tyler Durden), you can use cold reading to prove how you knew two women are best friends. When you're talking to them, ask an inane question like "What brand of toothpaste do you use?" And watch what happens. Because no matter what you ask them, two women will usually look at each other first before answering. And if they don't on your first question, just say, "Okaaaay . . . " like you are examining their answer, and ask another, like "Who is your favorite shoe designer?" At some point they *will* look at each other. As soon as they do, say "Stop! Did you guys notice you just looked at each other? That's how I know you're best friends. If you weren't, one of you, or both of you would have just looked straight ahead at me and answered." This is usually followed with them hugging each other, and seeing you as the hero who cemented their friendship. From here you can roll into a story or just about anything.

PROPS

Calm down, I'm not going to recommend you pull a Carrot Top and lug a duffel bag full of crap with you into a bar. (Although guys have been known to do that.) What I am suggesting is, just like a ninja, you use anything at your disposal as a weapon.

Remember the role playing example in Chapter 7 where you took silly shirts and tried them on with your target? That shirt was a prop you grabbed because it was close at hand, and a funny and engaging story could be built around it. Get good at varying this depending on where you are. If you're in an office supply store and spot a hot babe shopping for file folders, grab a couple of pens. In a variation on an opinion opener, ask her which one looks better with your outfit. Hold each of them up, one at a time, while doing your best, over the top model poses. When she picks one, close by asking her to write down her number, so you can see how sexy it looks while she's writing with it.

One of my favorite uses of props comes from Mystery. As a fool-proof opener, he would walk up to a target, tilt his head to the side with a serious look on his face, and just stare at her. When she would look confused or ask "What do you want?" he'd smile and pull out a Pez dispenser. Which would usually get her to laugh and say something like, "I love Pez and haven't had any for years!" He'd offer her one, and she'd accept—because who ever turns down Pez? This gave him a perfect opener: "Didn't your mom ever warn you about taking candy from strangers?" She'll always answer, "Of course." He follows with, "And it's bad for your teeth . . . ." She agrees. Then he elevates and seals it with, "Isn't it funny how what's dangerous can be so fun and exciting?" before transitioning into another subject to build on the emotion he's just brought up, or else going right into a close.

But my all time favorite prop? A small vial of bubbles. If you want to be surrounded by excited women quickly, break this out and start blowing bubbles. No matter where you are—a bar, a mall, an elevator—it works every time. And the sex talk can be ramped up easily by bringing the "blowing" into play. (I bet Lawrence Welk got mad babes.)

GAMES

Here's an interesting paradox: Women hate when you play games with them. But they also *love* when you play games with them. They are not only a cunning adversary, but a confusing adversary as well. Let me explain. Women *hate* when men play head games with them; it's just never a good idea. But they *love* the fun games that you get them to play with you in a bar or club; these are always a good idea. See, women love to be challenged and they enjoy a little friendly competition. Games are a great way to build attraction and qualify her, without getting caught up in the small talk trap. They are also perfect for getting her to kiss you. Here are a few to try:

GETTING TO KNOW YOU GAME

If a woman starts down the "where are you from, what do you do, blah, blah, blah" path, stop her and ask her if she's ever played the Getting to Know You game. This was originally attributed to Mystery and has evolved over time, but it's basically small talk turned into a contest. The rules are you alternate questions, but they can't be yes or no questions. Anything is fair game, no matter how personal. You must answer or you lose and have to do something for the other person, like buy them a drink or give them a ten-minute neck massage. Start slow and innocent and gradually build into more personal and sexual questions. You'll be amazed at how much intimate info a woman will give up under the guise of winning a game. You'll have no problem telling when she's getting turned on and, when she is, your final question is "Do you want to kiss me?" I don't have to tell you what her answer usually is.

THE LYING GAME

Another game that's good when the conversation starts to lull and it seems like small talk is right around the corner is the Lying Game. Tell her instead of answering with the real answer, you both have to come up with the most ridiculous, outrageous lies you can think of. There's no such thing as too far-fetched; the bigger the lie, the better. She'll have a great time thinking up completely fantastic answers to boring questions like, "Where are you from?" and "Do you have any pets?" And it gives you a chance to showcase your creativity and humor. The bonus? Ramping up the sexuality is no problem, because she's "lying" about her answers anyway. Any stigma or embarrassment she would normally attach to them are erased. So go ahead and ask her to describe the craziest sex position she's ever tried, or the craziest place she's ever done it. Then ask her if she wants to kiss you. At this point in the game a yes is a yes, and so is a no. You win either way.

THE "WOULD YOU?" GAME

Remember the movie *Indecent Proposal*, where Demi Moore played a married woman who agrees to have sex with Robert Redford's character for $1 million? So does the woman you're picking up. So start the game by asking her if she would have accepted that proposal. Then ask how much money it would take for her to do all kinds of things: paint your house, jump out of a cake at a party, have sex with a stranger . . . and then start negotiating her price and joke that you are going to go around the bar and raise the money to get her to do it.

KISSING BET

This isn't really a game per se, but it is a great way to build sexual tension and get her to kiss you. After you've been talking to her for a while and have some attraction going, tell her you know a really cool bar bet that wins you money every time. Bet her $1 you can kiss her right on the mouth, without using your lips or tongue. She'll tell you that's impossible. You say it absolutely *can* be done. Let the debate go on for a few minutes, and even tell her you're willing to go double or nothing to prove you can do it. When she finally takes the bet, make a big production about getting ready. Put a $1 bill on the table. Have her do the same. Then look her in the eyes, and gradually get closer to her lips. Keep going closer and closer. Finally, when you are just about touching her lips, go in and give her a long passionate kiss. Then tell her it was the best $1 you've ever spent.

POINTS

This isn't a game in the traditional sense, but it's one you can assume you're both already playing without you ever asking her to join in. Here's what I mean: For everything she does that you like, assign it points. If she mentions something about sports, say "A sports fan! I love that. You get 100 points." If she makes a comment about another chick's outfit, "That's the funniest, bitchiest thing I've heard all night, 250 points!" It doesn't matter what the points are for, you are getting her to qualify herself, and you're building higher value. Eventually she'll ask you what the points are for and the real fun begins. You can assign point values to anything that involves the two of you. Simply earning points is another form of chick crack, thanks to those sex and relationship tests in women's magazines. Finally, a reason to like *Cosmo*.

ROLE PLAYING

You know how women just love fantasy? (Seriously, anyone who can sit through those *Twilight* movies has got to love fantasy.) Well they love it even more when it revolves around them. And when you insert her into a fantasy that's fun, exciting, outrageous, silly, and also includes you, she'll associate you with fun and exciting things. Remember that Bank Robber opener I mentioned in Chapter 5, where you ask a pair of girls to be the drivers for a bank heist you're planning? That's a great role play. Even though it's completely outrageous to believe you are really going to rob a bank, it projects excitement and fun onto the two of you being together.

Another popular role-play is to tell her you are running away together to Las Vegas to get married. The details you can discuss are endless, from whether you'd rather have Elvis or Cher marry you, should she wear a white dress or sexy lingerie, should you drive up or parachute in, it just goes on and on. Plus, you can ramp up the sexuality by talking about the honeymoon, and what you plan on doing. "I've booked the Horny-moon suite at the Shangri-La Hotel just off the Strip. It has a rotating round bed and a champagne-shaped hot tub . . . ." And, should you separate during the course of the night, you can always come back to her once in a while and say something like "Don't forget, we have a 2 A.M. flight to Vegas. The Little Chapel of Love won't give me my deposit back, so don't be late." Even if some other guy is trying to worm his way in there, bringing that up will trigger how much fun she had with you.

And role playing doesn't have to be limited to one on one. You can jump into a group of women and get them all going at once. Tell them you've decided that they are now your groupies and go into all the things you expect your groupies to do for you. Another one of my favorites is to tell the group that you've decided to make them your bodyguards. They're now responsible to walk you through crowds and take out people who try to get too close—just like you're the President. Only you want them to run alongside your limo in high heels and lingerie, and you'll call them your Victoria's Secret Service.

CAT STRING THEORY

Have you ever played with a cat with a piece of string? If yes, you've probably noticed that when you keep pulling the string away the cat goes after it, over and over, as long as you keep putting the string in reach and then pulling it away. The minute you keep the string in one spot the cat gets bored. Quickly. Well, Cat String Theory says that women behave exactly the same way with men. The second you show a woman that you're all hers she loses interest. This is where "Nice Guys" fail miserably. They lie down and do everything for a woman from the minute they meet and show her how unrelentingly attracted they are. And there's no fun in that for her. No drama. No tension. And just like the cat, she quickly loses interest.

So how do you avoid becoming a "dead string?" By employing the Push/Pull technique. This is where you give her some attention (push), and then pull back a little. Give a little more attention, and then ignore her for a bit. Tell her you think she'd be the perfect girl for you, and then ask if she can cook, because you can't date a girl who can't even boil water. If she says of course she can cook, ask her what her favorite dish is to prepare. Whatever it is, it's not exactly your favorite. Can she cook anything else? You hope so because you can't be dating a one-dish girl. Oh, she's a gourmet cook? Well then it's back on. But wait, isn't gourmet food fattening? You can't eat all that rich food, it will ruin your physique . . . and on and on it goes. Dangle the string. Pull it back. All that tension and suspense will keep her interested. A word of caution though: Overdoing it can be tiring and annoying, and too much push without enough pull can make you seem impossible to attain, both of which will make her lose interest. So keep a close eye on her reactions; if she starts drifting over toward angry, it's time to add a lot more push.

SCARCITY

Have you ever had too much of a good thing? I have. I put myself through college working in a pizzeria and one of the perks was free pizza for employees. As a result I had one of my favorite foods for dinner six or seven nights a week. After a couple of weeks, I couldn't even look at a pie. I'd had enough.

That doesn't just apply to food, but to people and relationships too. If you are always around your girl, she's going to start to feel the same way about you; it's just part of human nature. Plus, if she knows that you'll pick up no matter when she calls, or if she says she's bored you'll come running over, she'll start to take you for granted.

Forget that. You're a guy who leads a busy life with a packed social calendar. She wants you to come over for a movie? "Sorry, I have plans tonight, but Thursday works. Let's do it then." It's an old restaurant trick to tell someone who calls for a reservation that the first time they request (and in some cases the second and third, too), is booked solid, but they can fit you in an hour or two later. Even if the place is empty. Why? Because that scarcity creates desire; it makes it seem like everyone wants in, which offers up a challenge.

If you have that same scarcity, you create that same sense of desire. So don't say things like, "Sure we can do that whenever you want, I'll make myself available." or "Let me know the best time for you" because busy guys only have certain windows available. Guys who have nothing better to do, no other friends, no other women, and no other social options, sit around waiting for the phone to ring. Think about your impression of a chick who always answered the phone when you called, never had anything going on, and was free just about any time you asked. Wouldn't you think, "hmmm, maybe she's desperate. Maybe she doesn't have any friends." And would you wonder if she had anything else going on in her life? Sure you would. And she'll think the same about you. Remember, you have an exciting life to live, and she's invited along as a guest. Don't make it seem as though she needs to rescue you from your boring life.

This also means that you shouldn't feel the need to answer the phone every single time you see her name on caller ID. She can leave a voicemail, and you'll get back to her when you're free. You don't want her to think you're watching the phone, waiting to hear her voice. You want to have an air of unpredictability; she can't always reach you when she wants to. So make her fight for your attention because if you've done your job right building attraction, she won't want to miss out on the incredibly fun times she associates with you.

CELL PHONE AS A WEAPON

Speaking of phone calls, a lot of guys, me included, have been very successful using the phone as a tool for building attraction and sealing the deal. Doing things like grabbing her phone and programming in your number so your name comes up when you call, work wonders. It also allows you to use one of my favorite inventions ever: texting. Believe the stuff women say about hating when guys text them instead of calling if you want, but in my experience it's invaluable for turning the conversation from safe to sexy.

I've found that woman behave differently when they feel protected by the screen. They can be someone else, let down some of their defenses, and say things they would never dare say to you over the phone or in person. Plus, you don't have to answer right away, which makes it easy to build suspense and tension. And since you can think your answers through completely before you answer, you don't have to be as "on your toes" to be clever and entertaining as you would have to be in person.

Quick tip for when you get her voicemail: There's a lot of debate about whether you should leave a voicemail or just try back later when a girl doesn't answer. No one ever seems to sound good on voicemails and you usually end up sounding needy: "Hi. It's me. Guess you're not there. Sorry I missed you. Call me back . . . ." It's painful to even type that. No wonder she's not calling you back. Instead, leave a partial story on her machine that is so compelling, she has to call you back to hear it, "Hey beautiful, I had this ridiculous dream about you last night. We were having dinner at this restaurant and a clown came up and did this insane thing to you. You gotta hear this." And hang up. She'll call back just to hear the ending. And since it was a "dream" you can make up anything you want. Then tell her to come meet you for drinks.

WAR STORY: THEY THOUGHT IT WAS ABOUT PUBLIC HUMILIATION. AND THEN THEY GOT LAID.

I've seen the use of gimmicks, props, and role-playing at work first hand. And work like a charm . . .

Now, I'm not saying it was *my* fraternity, but I have heard stories of a certain fraternity making their pledges go out to bars

dressed in outlandish costumes during Hell Week. Bunny suits. Pirate outfits. Diapers and baby bonnets. You name it, these guys were forced to wear it—and then go out and have a few pitchers of beer at the most popular college bars.

The pledges would dread the impending embarrassment for weeks. Some guys would even drop right before the big night rather than face the embarrassment of having to roll mob deep dressed like it was Halloween at the insane asylum. Others would beg and plead for anything else they could do but suffer through that night. They thought we were subjecting them to public humiliation, but we knew different. Because year after year, pledge class after pledge class, the same thing happened: Those guys would almost all get laid that night. And if they didn't score that night, they'd end up with a pocket full of phone numbers for a shot at scoring another night.

Sure it was embarrassing to walk into a crowded bar in costume. And yeah groups of other guys would point and laugh and bust their balls without mercy. But the attention they got from chicks was incredible, which made absorbing all that abuse very, very worth it. All the girls wanted to dance with the six-foot-two Drag Queen. Or do shots with the Big Baby. Or snuggle up to Bugs Bunny. (Or Jessica Rabbit, depending on the mood of the brothers.). And it should be obvious by now that the reason they were so attracted to these guys was that they were not only showing incredible fearlessness by walking to a college bar dressed that way, but they were also highly entertaining and showed the girls an unforgettable time. They also displayed loyalty to each other and to the fraternity by going through with what was asked—even though it seemed demeaning and pointless at the time. It was the perfect storm of Attraction.

But what's not as obvious, and what the pledges didn't understand while sweating out Costume Night for weeks beforehand, was this: There is no better or easier opener than having a woman approach you. And while it may not work every day, standing in a bar wearing a bright pink bunny suit is a sure-fire way to get at least one woman to walk up and ask why the hell you're dressed like that. Have a great answer (and "I lost a bet" is not a great answer), and it's game on. Plus, having all the props that went along with their costumes provided perfect openers. Big Baby could tell a group of hot women it was feeding time and could they buy him a martini for his baby bottle. And hold it for him. The Drag Queen can ask a couple of gorgeous ladies at the bar for makeup tips. A Pirate could role play his ass off. So what these guys quickly learned was that we weren't trying to humiliate them. We were just showing them how much fun it could be to just drop all the self-consciousness and just enjoy the night—and bring along a bunch of ladies for the ride.

Sun Tzu said "In order to carry out an attack with fire, we must have means available; the material for raising fire should always be kept in readiness." And just like the dating ninja you're becoming, you increase your chances for a successful mission by keeping all those weapons at the ready—especially if you use the most powerful weapon of all, which you'll read about next.

- Sun Tzu didn't always use conventional weapons during battle. Sometimes the situation called for something a little more bad ass than the traditional: fire.
- Fire was Sun Tzu's version of shock and awe, and you have the dating equivalent of fire at your disposal. But you have to be careful never to overuse fire. Use it sparingly or risk (pardon the pun), burning it out.
- Some of the tricks and tactics in this chapter may seem corny and stupid, but all are field-tested and seriously effective. Some are real Evil Genius shit, so wield their power with caution.
- Some of the things you should add to your arsenal include:

1. **Gimmicks** like Palm reading, Astrology, Handwriting analysis and Psychic readings.
2. **Props** may seem silly, but things like Pez dispensers and bubbles work wonders at knocking down Bitch Shields.
3. **Games.** Women hate 'em, but they also love 'em. Get her to play with you and you're in.
4. **Role Playing.** Women just love fantasy, and when you weave a story that centers around her—and you—she'll associate you with fun and exciting things, which leaves her wanting more.
5. **Cell phones** can be one of your most effective weapons. For example, you can use texting to ramp up the sexual tension, because the safety of the screen lets her say things she never would in person.
6. **Sun Tzu** said the material for raising fire should always be kept in readiness. Make sure you have some of this "fire" at the ready when you and your buddies go out on a mission.

CHAPTER 13
THE USE OF SPIES

"Love takes hostages."

—Neil Gaiman, novelist

Sun Tzu says, "Knowledge of the spirit world is to be obtained by divination; information in natural science may be sought by inductive reasoning; the laws of the universe can be verified by mathematical calculation; but the disposition of the enemy are ascertainable through spies and spies alone."

Spies. They were his secret weapon, and they can be yours too. I'm not saying it's easy to flip a woman into becoming your spy, or that there aren't some pitfalls, but believe me, the rewards are worth the work you'll put in.

JAMES BOND USED PUSSY GALORE. YOU SHOULD TOO.

Think for a second about what happens when one woman sees you with another woman—especially a beautiful woman. There's an instant rise in your value. You all of a sudden become "safe" to talk to and more desired. It's part of human nature to want what someone else has, especially if you see how much they are enjoying it. And when a woman sees another woman enjoying the company of a particular man, she figures there must be something to him that's highly desirable. Case in point: Most women want their husbands to wear a wedding ring to signify that they're taken and to tell other women to keep their hands off. I have a buddy whose wife *doesn't* want him to wear a wedding ring for fear of attracting other women. She knows that it signals to other women that he doesn't have a problem with commitment and must have some seriously desirable qualities for another to want to lock him up for the rest of his life. You gotta love her thinking.

In addition, being seen with a beautiful woman shows that you are comfortable around hot women, and that they in turn are comfortable around you. She becomes your walking, talking testimonial, and this starts the wheels of curiosity turning in every other woman who sees you. Ever seen a dumpy guy walk into a club or restaurant with a really hot chick on his arm? After you get done gnawing on your arm in jealousy, you start asking yourself, what the fuck does that guy have that I don't? Is it money? Power? A ten-inch hog? It's always about what *he* has that got him the hot girl. Not "what's wrong with *her* that she had to stoop so low?"

It's no different with women. Walk into a bar with a hot chick who is having a great time with you, and every other woman in the place will want to know what it is about you that she sees. (And I haven't even mentioned that attractive women tend to have attractive friends, which not only multiplies the hot women you'll have around you, increasing your chances to meet women when you go out as a group, but also giving you an inside track to get to know *them* as possible dates. After all, you are friends with their friend. You must be a great guy.)

PUT *HER* MONEY WHERE HER MOUTH IS

So how do you score a female friend willing to go out with you while you use her to score other chicks? That's the tricky part. You might have a female you've been friends with for years, who is always saying she wishes you could find the right girl. Well, tell her to put her money where her mouth is and help you. Or maybe one of the women you approached that put you in the Friend Zone would make a good spy. I know I already said that being "just friends" with certain women isn't what you're looking for—especially if they're hot and you originally had intentions of hooking up with them—but like any rules, there are exceptions. If she agrees to wing you and knows what she's doing in that department, well you may as well install a revolving door on your bedroom.

LET HER PEEP-TOE PUMPS KICK OPEN SOME DOORS

If you have a great spy working with you, you no longer need openers. She is now your opener. You don't have to fear getting into a set. A great wingwoman (or Pivot, as she's sometimes called, because she lets you pivot around her to get to the target), is the golden key that opens all locks. Women don't generally put up their Bitch Shields when one of their own knocks at the gates and requests entry. You'll get in with the classic, "It's okay, he's with me" pass.

And once you're in, she'll laugh at all your jokes, encourage you to tell your best stories, and be perfectly comfortable letting you put your arm around her; all subliminal signals to the other women that you are high value, sexual, and desirable. She's able to plant seeds and knock down defensive walls with an ability and deftness that would crush the average wingman. Wait. Scratch that. That would crush even a wingman who is *well above average*. And there is always the strong possibility that when she sees you attracting other women, she'll reconsider her decision to just be friends. A win/win for you.

TAKE CARE OF YOUR PIVOT

But understand, in order to wing you properly, she has to know your secrets. She has to know your openers. She'll have heard your stories a dozen times or more, and will still laugh in all the right places. She'll play you up to your targets as the greatest catch this side of Clooney, even knowing your bad habits and flaws. And that's why Sun Tzu says, "There must be no more intimate relations in the whole army than those maintained with spies. No other relation should be more liberally rewarded." Since a solid pivot is one of the greatest weapons you have in your arsenal, you need to treat her like one. That means she gets taken care of before anyone else. The "Never buy drinks for a woman" rule does not apply to her. Ever. If she's feeding you hot prospects, and building you up in the process, you're feeding her drinks. And anything else she wants.

It goes back to the subject of Loyalty too. She's more than earned it, so that means when the phone rings at 8 A.M. on a Saturday because there's a sale she can't miss and her car is in the shop, you drag your sorry ass out of bed, no matter how hungover you are, and you take her. She's a valued asset. One you don't want to risk losing. As Sun Tzu tells us, "Spies are a most important element in war, because upon them depends an army's ability to move." And you definitely want to keep moving.

WAR STORY: THE ONE THAT GOT AWAY. AND STARTED IT ALL.

Ahab had his white whale. Don Quixote had his windmills. And I had the blonde in the luggage department . . .

Back when I had just graduated from college, I got a job as an executive in the restaurant department at Bloomingdale's flagship store in Manhattan. One of the restaurants I was in charge of running was way down on the subway level, right next to the luggage department. Far from the crowded main floors packed with model/actresses hawking cosmetics, the latest fashions and high-priced accessories to the rich and famous above us, this was not exactly the most exciting location. Which was okay with me, because I got to look out the entrance and see "Her" every day.

I say "Her" because I'm not sure I ever knew her name. I think I heard it once, but only after it was too late. So to me she was always The Blonde from Luggage. Not exactly the sexiest name, which was a shame because she deserved something more fitting.

She was young, petite, and absolutely beautiful. Not in the "I want to be a model" sense like all the other women who worked there—just a genuine, real beauty made up of loose blonde curls, big blue eyes, an easy smile—and a ridiculous body. She was the whole package and she intimidated the hell out of me. Sure I had dated a lot of girls in college, but back then it was mostly drunken frat house hookups, nothing that required a lot of skill or self-confidence. And at this point in my dating career, I had neither. My standard approach was to wait until a woman came to me, or made her attraction so obvious that I was finally comfortable enough to do something about it. Typical Average Frustrated Chump behavior.

And since The Blonde just smiled her friendly smile and didn't do much else, I admired her from inside of my restaurant, while taking my mind off her by dating several low-hanging fruit model wannabes who came in day after day flirting and looking for attention.

Then one day one of her coworkers came in for coffee and told me he needed it to beat down the hangover he was suffering through. He got it drinking heavily at the big party they had the night before to say goodbye to the Blonde from Luggage. "I'm sorry, what?!" was all I could get out. No more Blonde smiling at me from behind a display of leather roll-aways? That can't be possible.

But it was. He told me she got another, better, offer with greater growth potential, and she took it. Yesterday had been her last day. And that wasn't all. What he told me next made it infinitely worse. "Yeah, and she was really upset no one told you about the party. Dude, she's had a thing for you for like, forever." My heart fell into my balls. She had a thing for me? "Yup. Talked about you a lot. But she always saw you flirting with all the cosmetics girls, and she was too shy to come over." *She* was too shy to come talk to *me*? I asked him if he knew how to get in touch with her, and he didn't. Plus the new job was going to move her out of state. She was gone. Forever. And I never got the chance to know if she was the One. Or at least the One for Now.

It was right then that I realized it hurt way more knowing that I missed out on what could have been an incredible time with an incredible girl because I did absolutely nothing than it ever could have hurt if I had just approached her and been turned down. If I had known enough to see the signs that she was attracted, instead of making myself believe she was just being polite . . . . If I had approached her and had an actual conversation, instead of months of just smiling back and forth . . . . If I had employed spies and asked one of her coworkers for some of the intel they obviously had . . . . If I had done any of that, I would have known. And things might have been very different.

So I decided to never let that happen again. And ever since that time, if I see a woman I want, I approach her. If there's no attraction, no big deal, I move on. But I don't plan on ever letting another one get away.

- According to Sun Tzu, the only way to learn about the enemy is through the use of spies—and using a woman as your "spy" can be incredibly valuable.
- Being seen with a beautiful woman instantly increases your value in the eyes of other women.
- You become "safe" to talk to and you show others that you are comfortable around hot women. Your spy actually becomes your walking, talking testimonial.
- You also arouse the curiosity of everyone who sees you. People who see a man with a hot woman automatically want to know what he has that attracted her.
- If you get an attractive female friend to agree to wing you, you might as well put a revolving door on your bedroom because she'll open doors and knock down defensive walls that a male wing could never dream of touching.
- In exchange, she gets better treatment, and is rewarded more, than any of your friends. She's earned your loyalty.

CONCLUSION

"The art of war is of vital importance to the state. It is a matter of life and death, a road either to safety or to ruin. Hence under no circumstances can it be neglected . . . ."

—Sun Tzu

"So . . . am I in it?"

That was the first thing every women said when I told them I was writing this book. The short answer I gave the majority of them was "No." The long answer for them all is "Absolutely." Because every approach I've ever made, every blow off I've ever been on the receiving end of, every girl I've ever hooked up with, and every relationship I've ever been in—the good, the bad, and the downright ugly—have made me who I am now. I learned something from all of them, no matter how painful (or costly) those lessons were. And that's how you have to look at the missions you're going to embark on. You may not always win the battle, but you can use what you learn from every outcome to help you win the war.

The typical battle Sun Tzu fought ended with him defeating his enemy, usually by capturing them, then taking their land, supplies, and treasure. In your case, a successful mission ends with a "close," meaning you asked for and received a kiss, phone number, email address, hand job, dinner date, or sheet partner. That was your ultimate goal. And it's usually how victories are scored.

But in all honesty, it doesn't matter if all you got out of the night was an interesting conversation with a woman. It beats the shit out of standing in the corner alone—or being home on the couch watching a *Burn Notice* marathon. If you've been out of the game for a while, or rarely ever went out to a club and spent time talking to a hot girl, that step alone is a big victory.

Shit Tests? Now you know they're nothing personal. They're just part of her make up, and you'll be hit with them all day long. Bitch Shields? You should have enough ammo to plow through the toughest of them. Intimidating gorgeous women? They're just like every other girl, and approaching shouldn't cause you an ounce of anxiety.

Sun Tzu gave us the rules to achieving victory on the battlefield; each step tested and proven. He made his soldiers not just better warriors, but better men. His rules were—and are—rules to live by not just for a pick up, but for life in general. They can, and maybe already have, made you a better man who has the confidence to go after whatever he wants, the awareness of what it takes to succeed, and the knowledge and ability to make it all happen.

So whatever battlefield you find yourself on, remember Sun Tzu's words: "The true object of war is peace." Or in this case, getting a piece. So put the book down, suit up, and go see if you can get into a few close quarters battles of your own. Have fun.

GLOSSARY

ALPHA OR ALPHA MALE

A guy who displays traits favorable to women and who is usually in charge of the social situation. Taken from the animal kingdom, where the strongest one of the group rules.

AFC (AVERAGE FRUSTRATED CHUMP)

A guy with no seduction skills. Usually displays "Nice Guy" behavior to women he is trying to hook up with. Coined by Ross Jefferies of Speed Seduction.

ATTRACTION (OPPOSED TO SEDUCTION)

Where you display the characteristics that women find attractive, to get them to become interested in you.

BITCH SHIELD

The rude or nasty behavior a woman uses to ward off guys she thinks are hitting on her.

BOREFRIEND

What you call the guy your target is currently dating.

CLOSE

To complete your mission. Can be a Kiss Close, an E-Mail Close, Number Close, Date Close, Fuck Close, etc.

COCKBLOCK

When someone consciously tries to prevent you from successfully picking up a woman, either to get the target himself, or just to watch you get shot down. Those who engage in this unforgivable behavior are known as Cockblockers. (Note: The gender flip of this is the Rack Jack, when someone prevents a woman from picking up a guy.)

DANCING MONKEY

A guy who acts like a fool in order to make women laugh, mistakenly thinking he is attracting them.

DOUCHEBAGGERY

Assorted antics perpetrated by douche bags to try to trick women into bed. Usually accompanied by a complete lack of morals, social skills, and any sense of style.

DRINK SHIELD

Body language where people hold their drinks in front of their chests to defend against social interactions. Displays insecurity to women.

GET OVER

To put something over on someone for your own gain. See Douchebaggery.

GEOGRAPHIC HOMOPHOBIA

The misguided idea that there are certain places no straight guy would ever be caught dead in. Like a dance class, wine bar, or art gallery.

GOOD GIRL DEFENSE/ANTI-SLUT DEFENSE
The resistance a woman puts up when she thinks the behavior you're engaging in would make her a "slut."

GRENADE
Similar to a Cockblocker, the Grenade is the person in the group with the ability to blow your whole mission to pieces.

HIRED GUNS
Women who are paid to be nice to you, like hostesses, waitresses, bartenders, and strippers.

JIM BELUSHI EFFECT
My term for the sitcom world's insistence that hot women go for goofy, inept men.

KINO
When a woman touches you during your conversation. Indicates she's interested in you. Coined by Ross Jefferies of Speed Seduction.

MOODLE
A Man Poodle. A poor bastard who has gone above and beyond just being a "Nice Guy" (See Nice Guy) and might as well be wearing a rhinestone studded collar. From the movie *She's Out of My League.*

NEG

A slightly negative comment, or offhanded compliment, said to a woman to show her you're not intimidated or impressed by her beauty. Coined by Mystery.

NICE GUY

A guy with little or no skills in dealing with women, he does everything he can in the mistaken belief that getting them to like him will result in them wanting to date him. Can usually be found most nights at home, on his couch, alone, waiting for her to call.

OBSTACLES

Anyone who can get in the way of you completing a successful mission: Cockblocker, Mother Hen, Mother Bear, Boyfriend, etc. Coined by Mystery.

ONE-ITIS

The debilitating notion that one woman is the only one for you. Can lead to crippling behavior. Coined by Mystery.

PEACOCKING

Wearing outrageous clothing and accessories to stand out from everyone else and grab attention.

PIVOT

A female wingman. She not only can open more doors than a male wingman, but she also offers tremendous Social Proof. (See entry.)

SEDUCTION (OPPOSED TO ATTRACTION)
Where you attempt to persuade a woman into bed, rather than get her to be attracted to you.

SET
The group of people you are interacting with while attempting to attract your target. A set can be made of any number of people. A single woman would be referred to as a "one set," a pair of women a "two set," etc.

SHIT TEST
Something a woman says or does to a guy to gauge a his reaction.

SOCIAL PROOF
First coined by psychologist Robert Cialdini, social proof is when your value is raised in other people's eyes simply due to the people you have around you. In the pick up world, being seen with beautiful woman makes you more desirable to other beautiful women.

TARGET
The woman you are ultimately after during your interaction with a set.

WINGMAN
The guy who has your back on all your missions. His job is to make sure you succeed.

INDEX

ABOUT THE AUTHOR

Eric Rogell is the guy behind TheBachelorGuy.com, the go-to resource for everyday men who want to elevate themselves above Neanderthal status—without going so far as to apply spray tanner before bed. He gives guys access and advice on the latest in gear, gadgets, grooming, cars, sports, and, of course, women.

Though he's been called a "major influencer" among men aged twenty-one to forty-five, and travels the world experiencing and reviewing products from companies like GM, Mazda, Gillette, and more liquor producers than he'd care to admit, Rogell's proudest moment came when he was dubbed "Maxim 2.0" by Olivia Munn on G4's *Attack of the Show.*

When he's not test driving the latest sports car or sampling a rare single malt, he writes and lectures on interactive marketing and social media, and is preparing a nationwide series of cooking classes for guys. Because the quickest way to the bedroom is through the kitchen.

He's a much-decorated veteran of the dating war and has been captured by the enemy—twice. (Fortunately he escaped both times.)